D1083347

KEATS SHELLEY & ROME

KEATS SHELLEY & ROME

An Illustrated Miscellany

———————————— ● ————————————

Compiled by
NEVILLE ROGERS

Postscript by
FIELD-MARSHAL EARL WAVELL
P.C., G.C.B., G.C.S.I., G.C.I.E., M.C.

Published on behalf of the
KEATS SHELLEY MEMORIAL ASSOCIATION

JOHNSON
LONDON

First Published 1949
Second Edition 1957
Third Edition 1963
Fourth Edition 1970

ISBN 0 65307 050 4

PRINTED IN GREAT BRITAIN BY
BILLING AND SONS LIMITED
GUILDFORD AND LONDON FOR
JOHNSON PUBLICATIONS LTD.
11-14 STANHOPE MEWS WEST, LONDON, S.W.7

CONTENTS

LIST OF ILLUSTRATIONS

TO
YOUNG ENGLISHMEN WHO DIED IN ITALY

COMPILER'S FOREWORD

MANY, like the compiler of these pages, will have felt recently in Italy something of the spell of the two poets whose roads led them, so differently, to Rome: for others the quiet house in the Piazza di Spagna provided something, at least, of England—a refuge where men could read and write and reflect, recovering for the moment an identity which had seemed lost amid the lunacy without. All these will remember the Memorial; they will remember too the welcome of that serene Italian lady its Curator, the friend of English poets and soldiers and a redoubtable foe to all who would disturb the peace of an Englishman's Roman treasure.

Here then is our theme: related to it there is a purpose. That purpose is to assist in the efforts which are being made to preserve the Keats-Shelley Memorial—now more than ever the symbol of so much and to so many.

NEVILLE ROGERS.

Hampstead, 1948.

PREFACE TO SECOND EDITION

MORE than ten years have passed since I compiled this book. Now, as it goes into a second edition, I would offer thanks to all whose interest has made it a regular source of income to the Keats-Shelley Memorial in Rome, then threatened with extinction by the results of war, but rejoicing this year in the fiftieth anniversary of its foundation. Much has been achieved in ten years, including the setting in order of the graves of Keats, Shelley, Severn and Trelawny and the repair and replenishing of the house and library in Piazza di Spagna. The full tale of all this has been told in the Annual Reports of the Keats-Shelley Memorial Association, compiled for the British Committee by Miss Elsa Forman, and in the Preface written by Miss Dorothy Hewlett to *Keats-Shelley Memorial Bulletin III*.

It is a tale of long labour and co-operation between Lady Crewe and her British Committee, the Committee in Rome, under the chairmanship of H.E. The British Ambassador, and the Keats-Shelley Association of America, under their late, beloved President, Miss Ruth Draper. Nor could these endeavours have been carried out without the energy, tact and devotion of our reliable Italian friend, Signora Vera Cacciatore.

The Memorial is safe for the moment but its future must be secured. An endowment fund has been started and its needs are considerable. I hope that the second edition of this miscellany may continue, like the first, to make some contribution.

NEVILLE ROGERS.

University of Birmingham,
1957.

PREFACE TO THIRD EDITION

SINCE my first edition appeared some fifteen years have gone by and much that was then topical has passed into history. By the 'fifties, as I noted in the Preface to my second edition, the Keats-Shelley Memorial had already passed out of its desperate situation of the 'forties into a new life of continuous, creative, activity. The 'sixties have seen no slackening either of our work or of the happy co-operation which makes it possible. Meanwhile from the outer world with its new struggles, people still come to Piazza di Spagna, as did my friend Shan Sedgwick in war-time, for a moment of "quiet, peace, pause in our lives"; and many of them, taking away this book, have been glad to contribute their help to the Endowment Fund of the Memorial to which, likewise, all royalties on its sales elsewhere will continue to be devoted. And if I make no apology in offering a third edition that is practically unchanged from its predecessors this is because I like to remember the kind comment of one of my contributors, that the book "catches the mood of liberation". Today, I feel, there will be no need for anybody to apologise for anything that has a chance of catching that mood as it flies.

Brandeis University　　　　　　　　　　　　　　　NEVILLE ROGERS.
Waltham, Mass., U.S.A.
1966

PREFACE TO FOURTH EDITION

THE editions mark the years . . . ten, fifteen, twenty—now twenty-five . . . *nec pietas moram*! Yet still, as on that momentous June morning, a quarter of a century ago, "The Memorial Stands". Still the visitors come. And still they take away copies of this little book, thereby contributing to its needs which, in an ever needier world, do not grow less.

In my fourth edition there is but one major change: the substitution (p. 49) of my own translation of Rilke's poem for that of J. B. Leishman. This new attempt to translate an almost untranslatable poem would not have been made without the encouragement of my late, ever-generous, friend; to him and to the Hogarth Press, I owe acknowledgment both for permission to publish it and for certain touches which I have gratefully borrowed from his version. A cognate acknowledgment would not, I think, be out of place to my friend Edoardo Cacciatore, that true poet whose *giudizi* have long been quietly at the service of the Memorial: he it was who, in days long distant, first drew my attention to Rilke's lines. And another acknowledgment, long overdue, should now be added: to the firm of Johnson, whose fourth edition is a memorial to its own faith in poets—a faith that dates from its readiness, even in the post-war days of paper shortage, to take a risk on our behalf.

Ohio University　　　　　　　　　　　　　　　NEVILLE ROGERS.
Athens, Ohio, 45701, U.S.A.
1969

ACKNOWLEDGMENTS

T HIS little book could not have been compiled without the patient help and kindly criticism of Miss Dorothy Hewlett. Mr. Edmund Blunden, at whose suggestion it was prepared, has been ready at all times with advice and encouragement. The thanks of the compiler and of the Keats-Shelley Memorial Association are due to Lord Wavell, who at a busy and critical moment in the affairs of an empire yet found time to honour poets, and to all those who have so kindly and generously contributed their work: my desert friend, Mr. A. C. Sedgwick; Signor Severini; Mr. Blunden and Miss Hewlett; Mr. Maurice Buxton Forman. Mr. Forman has allowed me the privilege of using a hitherto unpublished portrait of Keats by B. R. Haydon. Reproduction of a water-colour painting of Shelley's house at Lerici is made by permission of the Hampstead Corporation, who have allowed me, also, the use of a poem by the late Lord Rennell of Rodd from their *John Keats: Memorial Volume*. A quotation from *Garibaldi's Defence of the Roman Republic* has been made by the kindness of the Master of Trinity and Messrs. Longmans Green; and to Miss Ruth Draper and Messrs. Faber and Faber I am indebted for leave to quote and to translate from the works of Lauro de Bosis. Thanks are due to Il Vittoriale degli Italiani for allowing translation of a passage from d'Annunzio's *Il Piacere;* my translation of Rilke's poem "Zu der Zeichnung, John Keats in Tode darstellend" has been made by permission of the Hogarth Press. If by inadvertence any other copyright material has been used apologies are tendered in advance to those concerned.

To Signora Signorelli Cacciatore, Curator of the Keats-Shelley Memorial, I am indebted not only for her direct contribution to the book but for much information and correspondence. Miss Ruth Draper, Mr. Force Stead, Mr. Ward Perkins and Miss Elsa Forman have read the manuscript and made useful criticism; Mr. Norman Kilgour and Mr. Harold Preston have given generously of their time and trouble; valuable too has been the interest of the Poetry Society. To all of these I tender my grateful thanks.

NEVILLE ROGERS.

THE SPANISH STEPS

THE KEATS-SHELLEY HOUSE

ROME 1909

An old-world house with rusted orange walls,
    Where, in the city's heart, you hear the drip
Of Sabine water plashing as it falls
    Into the marble semblance of a ship:
Its windows open on a giant stair
    Crowned by an obelisk, and higher still
Sun-traced in Rome's gold-radiant air
    The Trinity that names the hill.

Enter the modest portal and ascend
    Those narrow steps where once with labouring breath
He came at even and the journey's end
    Who seeking life was greeted here by death.
The marble stairs are steep, the shade strikes cold
    In midmost summer. Fling the window wide
And let the Roman sun flood in. Behold
    The place where Adonais died.

Little is changed. The lime-washed walls enclose
    A narrow chamber, with a roof pale blue
Between the rafters, panelled for the rose
    In mock relief that once his wide eyes knew,
Sleeplessly watching till the drooped lids tired:
    A red-tiled floor, and windows whence at times
The lilt of the great city's life inspired
    Suggestion of unwritten rhymes.

And this was all he knew of that great Rome,
    The deathless mother of immortal men,
Dreamed of in visions in his Northern home,
    And reached at last, and still beyond his ken:
A window world—blue noon and even's glow,
    The passing pageant of the Spanish Square,
And blown from baskets on the steps below
    The scent of violets in the air.

15

And here, above yon rampired stairway oft
   Mounting at eve would Shelley pause to gaze
Where the great dome left earth to soar aloft
   A glory centred in a crimson blaze.
And Byron's shadow haunts this Spanish place;—
   Those were his windows, where the master brain
Divined the soul behind the marble face
   And made the dead Rome live again.

And therefore men from either side the sea
   Who speak the same great language, joining hands,
Designed the poet's house of death to be
   A pilgrim shrine for poets of their lands.
So keep, my country, as a holy trust
   The house we tended with our love and care!
Their ashes mix with Rome's immortal dust,
   But in the spirit they are there.

LORD RENNELL OF RODD.

HEAD OF JOHN KEATS
from a drawing by Joseph Severn

Your sincere friend
John Keats.

From a drawing by Joseph Severn in the Victoria and
Albert Museum

SHELLEY WRITING "PROMETHEUS UNBOUND" IN THE BATHS OF
CARACALLA

from a posthumous portrait by Joseph Severn. In the Keats-
Shelley Memorial House, Rome.

THE MEMORIAL STANDS

ROME 1944

T H E R E was to be a great deal more fighting. The decisive phase had not yet been reached. The attack in Northern France, which actually began on the morrow, was awaited: none knew how it would prosper. Yet for us, or some of us, who entered Rome with the Allied columns that bright morning, 5th June, 1944, there was a surprise emotion in so abrupt a descent of peace.

Rome, during the years of world-madness, had, perhaps for the only time in all her venerable history, lapsed from being a world-city, and instead had become merely the capital of one country— a country that because of a silly whim had decided to wage war against us.

Rome conquered at last was Rome instantaneously restored: Rome taken was Rome, handed back. In one spot, anyway, on this warring and war-torn planet things were once more as they should be. With time over whose healing process Rome seemed to have a monopoly the recent regrettable past would soon be fused with other tragic episodes generally lamented by the very stones.

My good companion Captain Mason, attached to British Army Public Relations, had the imagination to halt our jeep on the Piazza di Spagna. I think it was the first time he had ever seen it. For me it was familiar from childhood. I believe, had times been normal and had I arrived in Rome by train, I should have come to this scene of touching beauty directly from the railroad station to look about me and to visit the Keats-Shelley Museum which adjoins it.

For the Keats-Shelley House is less of a museum than a house of contemplation, itself brooding inwardly upon its tenant the poet who died in one of its rooms about a century and a quarter before, and outwardly upon the very view which was before his eyes during the last days of his sad life.

We climbed the stairs. The Italian Curator whom we were to find refreshing and charming company, came to the door in delayed response to our knocking and opened it cautiously. I believe we were the first in four years who sought entrance, not to loot or to search for incriminating documents, but to peruse the wealth of material the house has to offer—things that can be carried away only in the spirit.

There, intact, were various objects all familiar. The furnishings were as they used to be. Severn's little study of the dying Keats was in place and there too was Severn's portrait of Shelley sitting among ruins, lost in the world he was in the very process of constructing. There was the smell—more of England than of Italy, or so one thinks—of leather bindings that bewitched Henry James. There was quiet, peace, pause in our lives in which to think, reflect and be thankful that such a haven had been spared, it would appear, by a miracle. Outside—it seemed very far away—we heard the clatter of our mechanized cavalry.

A. C. SEDGWICK
(*New York Times* Correspondent, attached
to the American Fifth Army.)

KEATS SHELLEY AND ROME

1816–22

"**M**OST of us, when we visit Rome, go up on the morning after our arrival to the heights of the Janiculum, and, standing on the terrace in front of San Pietro in Montorio, look back across the Tiber at the city spread beneath our feet in all its mellow tints of white, and red, and brown, broken here and there by masses of dark green pine and cypress, and by shining cupolas raised to the sun. There it all lies beneath us, the heart of Europe and the living chronicle of man's long march to civilization: for there, we know, are the well-proportioned piazzas with their ancient columns and their fountains splashing in shade and shine around the sculptured water-gods of the Renaissance; the Forum won back by the spade; and the first monuments of the Christian Conquest. There rise the naked hulks of giant ruins stripped of their imperial grandeur long ago by hungry generations of Papal architects; and there, on the outskirts of the town, is the Pyramid that keeps watch over the graves. As we look down we feel the presence of all the centuries of European history, a score of civilizations dead and lying in state one beside the other; and in the midst of their eternal monuments mankind still swarms and labours, after all its strange and varied experience, still intent to live, still busily weaving the remote future out of the immemorial past."

G. M. TREVELYAN

(Garibaldi's Defence of the Roman Republic.)

A whole century has passed since the eyes of Europe were fixed on Garibaldi's Roman Republic, and since our English historian looked from the Janiculum, Rome has known struggles as bitter and as significant to mankind as any evoked in his memorable pages. Yet we may look down still on the unchanged wonders, and there on the outskirts the pyramid keeps watch, undisturbed, though narrowly, by a near-falling bomb.

Nor have the times wholly changed since the second decade of the nineteenth century when there came to Rome the two young English poets who were to have their place among the "eternal monuments". Were they alive to-day Keats and Shelley might find much that was familiar in the general outlines of our world. They looked as we do upon a Europe recently emerged from a weary struggle and beheld as we do the apparently rapid descent from victory into disunion of nations united in war. Everywhere, at home and abroad, rulers were threatening new servitudes in the guise of new freedoms and, amid a conflict of fears and ambitions, hope and despair alternated and intermingled on a background of suffering and disorder. The dawn of nineteenth century Liberalism was awaited. Dimly distant still lay freedom, humanity and the beauty which was truth.

Shelley's last voyage was in the same year as Garibaldi's first: Keats had died in the previous year and, two or three months after him, Napoleon. It was in the world between worlds that the poets' paths crossed and led to Rome: that world of theirs is reflected in their poetry and in their lives, and the reflections are bright to-day. Different enough as writers and as men, they lived differently too, but they brought alike into the art of living resources of genius and of humanity seldom seen in any age. Common to both—and not least among their qualities which call out to us across the years—was a virility and a whole-heartedness marking all that they ever wrote or did.

Born of the "ruling classes" Shelley had in superabundant measure that sense of responsibility which, if sometimes obscured, has always been ready to break out among Englishmen of his order, driving them in various ways to make their various marks upon the world. This sense and its accompanying impulse might well have made of him a discoverer of new lands within the physical world or a ruler of old: instead it made him a rebel against the systems of his day. So closely indeed was he concerned at all times with the reformation of the early nineteenth century that from a first reading of his biographers the wonder might arise how the reformer within Shelley left room for the poet. Both, in fact, were integral parts of the same powerful and highly-geared machine and both driven by the same electrical energy. The struggles of Shelley the reformer—his crusades for civil and religious liberty, his youthful pamphleteering, his quixotic philanthropy—were born in the essential mind of Shelley the poet.

That mind was Greek and all-embracing. Together with art and the well-being of society he had an interest in science extending far beyond the normal contemporary limitations. All-embracing too were the connotations of that ancient word: no more for him than for Lucretius did they exclude poetry and they comprehended, indeed, the whole range of human knowledge and experience. With the Romantic Movement what Victor Hugo called "Liberalism in Art" had preceded Liberalism in politics. For Shelley the freedom of mankind began with the freedom of thought. Herein is his message to-day. Indeed the very words of a broadcast message of His Majesty the King are curiously anticipated in the preface to *Prometheus Unbound*.[1]

"The great writers of our own age are, we have reason to suppose, the companions and forerunners of some unimagined change in our social condition or the opinions which cement it. The cloud of mind is discharging its collected lightning, and the equilibrium between institutions and opinions is now restoring, or is about to be restored."

Commenting on the passage Shelley's latest biographer[2] remarks that the poet when he wrote was conscious of what we now see in our daily lives and proceeds to a quotation from a lecture by Sir William Bragg:

"It is an important fact that Science advances over a wide front, and the various branches of it move on together: not absolutely keeping step with each other, but preserving a general line."

Akin to this is the metaphysical conception throughout the poem of Man's mission in the Universe: in the speech of Earth, for example, are summits from which the poet would seem to attain a prevision of the aeroplane and of the atomic era:

[1] "Opinion striking against opinion ignites the spark that can kindle the lamp of truth." H.M. The King, Christmas Day, 1946.
[2] Edmund Blunden. *Shelley*, Collins, 1946.

"The lighting is his slave; heaven's utmost deep
Gives up her stars, and like a flock of sheep
They pass before his eye, are numbered, and roll on!
The tempest is his steed, he strides the air;
And the abyss shouts from her depths laid bare,
Heaven, hast thou secrets? Man unveils me; I have none."

And in the preceding stanza we find lines which express, together with the Mission of Man, the mission of poet and of scientist—and of Shelley:

"All things confess his strength. Through the cold mass
Of marble and of colour his dreams pass;
Bright threads whence mothers weave the robes their
children wear."

Shelley came of a long-lived race, and it is tempting to speculate on the scope of the disaster which cut short in youth a life so full of varied promise.

From his combination of thought with practice, his Greek mind and his conception of science, many a "bright thread" might have been woven into the somewhat drab texture of Victorian materialism. In times when a new-born "education" was too frequently confused with information his passion for instructing others might have made him no less effectual a pioneer of "sweetness and light" than the poet and Inspector of Schools born in the year of his death. And it may well be, had he lived to inherit as a Sussex landowner, that he would have become a legislator like other Shelleys, inheriting at the same time that unfulfilled renown as an orator which was foreseen by more than one of his contemporaries. In the prefaces and elsewhere we may discern, perhaps, the utterance of a Burke or a Churchill, and certain it is that few even among our acknowledged legislators entertained a livelier sense than Matthew Arnold's "ineffectual angel" of what is now fashionably called a *théorie d'engagement*.

It cannot be said that we invariably find Keats "keeping step" with Shelley, nevertheless his thought is here and there found to be preserving the same general line. In May 1818, writing to his friend Reynolds of the poet's relation to contemporary life, he thus follows up an analysis of Milton and Wordsworth:

"What then is to be inferr'd? O many things—It proves there really is a grand march of intellect—It proves that a mighty providence subdues the mightiest Minds to the service of the time being, whether it be in human Knowledge or Religion."

That Keats had pondered more than he writes about "the general and gregarious advance of intellect" as contrasted with "individual greatness of mind" there are strong indications in the letter.

Earlier, in 1816, Keats had written in his world-between-worlds of what was to come and he was not to see:

"And other spirits there are standing apart
    Upon the forehead of the age to come;
These, these will give the world another heart,
    And other pulses. Hear ye not the hum
        Of mighty workings? ——
Listen awhile, ye nations, and be dumb."

Already there were born men who, in England and in other countries, were to give the world "another heart and other pulses". Dr. Trevelyan points out that one of the main pulses was to come from Italy, the land which Keats was to see but not to know. In an early sonnet he refers to his "languishment for skies Italian" and there is a passing interest perhaps in his intention, of which we learn from a contemporary, to go to South America and to "write a Poem on Liberty". It was in South America that the great heartener of Italy was to graduate as a Liberator: in 1816 Giuseppe Garibaldi was a nine-year-old sailor boy at Nice.

This was Keats, the youthful visionary of 1816, and we have seen the ripening thinker of two years later. By October 1818, we have a Keats matured still further. To his brother and sister-in-law in America he gives a picture of the contemporary scene which lacks nothing of interest for the modern reader:

"The worst thing he (Napoleon) has done is, that he has taught them to use their monstrous armies—The Emperor Alexander it is said intends to divide his Empire as did Diocletian—creating two Czars beside himself and continuing the Supreme Monarch of the whole—Should he do this and they for a series of Years keep peaceable among themselves, Russia may spread her conquest even to China. I think it a very likely thing that China itself may fall: Turkey certainly will. Meanwhile European North Russia will hold its horns against the rest of Europe, intriguing constantly with France. Dilke, whom you know to be a Godwin-perfectibility Man, pleases himself with the idea that America will be the country to take up the human intellect where England leaves off. . . ."

In observation and analysis, in manner as in method, this is typical of Keats and could never have been written by Shelley without endless searching after cause, effect and remedy. The two poets are no longer in line. For us the eternal youthfulness of Shelley's dreams and ardour forms much of his charm. But in the whole history of genius few have proceeded from youth to maturity with the same rapidity as did Keats between 1817 and 1819, and to him, already, Shelley's dreams may well have appeared a mere phase of youth. He himself had known such a phase, apologizing for it ingenuously in the preface to *Endymion*.

Here we come to an essential difference in outlook. Keats was no more than Shelley a poet of the Ivory Tower: he could survey the world abroad and at home and in his open admiration of Hunt and other persecuted Liberals he gave an earnest of his expressed wish to do something for the Liberal cause before he died. But Shelley's ideal of the poet's mission was not his. Realist as much as idealist, Keats could spare no time for Godwinian notions of Man's perfectibility, and in a world where the "Lion must starve as well as the swallow" he considered less how to solve than how to interpret the problems of life:

> ". . . . to bear all naked truths,
> And to envisage circumstance, all calm,
> That is the top of sovereignty."

Truth lay in the strange beauty of the struggle. This was the message both of the Greeks and of Shakespeare, and it is the message given by a Poet-Laureate in our own time:

"Our stability is but balance, and wisdom lies
In masterful administration of the unforeseen."

It is in his balanced wisdom that Keats appears the more modern man.[1]

The difference between the two poets' outlook upon life is one with their difference in poetic method. Shelley's genius was all-embracing. For Keats concentration and "intensity" were the essentials. Of Shakespeare he says—"He led a life of Allegory: his works are the comments on it" and his own life and works stand in a similar relationship. Concentration, of experience as well as intellect, and the protection of his receptive faculty ("Negative Capability" as he called it) against the impingement of things outside his scope were vital to his life and art. Writing to Shelley of this need for concentration he says that an artist must have "selfishness perhaps". He adds: "The thought of such discipline must fall like cold chains upon you, who perhaps never sat with your wings furled for six months together."

Behind the difference in outlook and in method lay a difference in circumstance. Born in surroundings less spacious if more harmonious than Shelley's, haunted by hereditary illness and the fear of an early death, he was struggling for survival like the field-mouse of whom he wrote, "the creature hath a purpose and its eyes are bright with it". Keats' purpose was to leave us what he could achieve while he lived of poetry worthy of his birthright. First and last for him came the mission of poetry and his own vocation as poet: Shelley's vital concern was the Mission of Man for which he longed with his poetry to be the trumpet. It is in his most admired work that Keats comes closest to his own ideal: of Shelley on the other hand it is probably true that his enchantment is most generally found in those poems where, abandoning tem-

[1] Though Shelley's later poems do reveal strong doubts of the perfectibility of man by social change. This almost unwilling evolution of the "millenium-dreaming mind" has been finely traced by Mr. John Lehmann. (See *Shelley in Italy*: John Lehmann, 1947.)

porarily the trumpet of the Mission of Man, he has allowed himself to be carried away by the "Spirit of Delight" and to become its lyre.

Keats was twenty-one and Shelley twenty-four when they first met. This was in the December of 1816 at Leigh Hunt's house in Hampstead. Keats was living happily with his brothers and his first book of poems was shortly to appear. A young man of the rising middle classes, less affluent for mysterious reasons than he should have been, he was forsaking medicine for poetry, and confident in his genius and his ambition, saw the world before him. Behind Shelley lay unhappiness at Eton and Oxford, quarrels with his family involving financial anxiety, and the tragic episode of the first marriage ending with Harriet's recent suicide. *Laon and Cythna*, *Queen Mab* and *Alastor* had been printed at his own expense. He had married Mary Godwin, daughter of the political philosopher whose "perfectability" notions were so deprecated by Keats. Shelley's liking for Keats was immediate. Keats, while admiring and liking Shelley, did not allow the relationship to become an intimate one. Other explanations apart, the real reason lay in the differences in outlook and poetic method. We may well accept Keats' own explanation: he refused to visit Shelley that he might have his "own unfettered scope". That scope left no room for shrilly-voiced expositions of the Mission of Man and, moreover, Shelley was far too strong and vivid a personality: in Keatsian phrase his "identity" pressed too hard upon an impressionable mind. Antagonism there was none but, psychologically, Keats required stimulus of another kind.

There is interest in the exchange of criticism and advice. During a walk on Hampstead Heath Shelley advised Keats, on the ground of their immaturity, not to publish his 1817 volume of poems—"my first blights". It was bold advice for the publication of this volume was an eagerly awaited event among all of Hunt's "Hampstead set". Nevertheless Keats was not annoyed and three years later reciprocated with great tact and good humour about the coming publication of *Prometheus Unbound*—"You, I am sure will forgive me for sincerely remarking that you might curb your magnanimity and be more of an artist, and load every rift of your subject with 'ore."

This was written in August 1820. Keats had gone far since 1817. Nevertheless he generously admits the justice of Shelley's advice even with reference to the great *Lamia* volume: "Most of the poems in the volume I now send you have been written above two years and would never have been published but for hope of gain; so you see I am inclined enough to take your advice now."

Be it noted that the criticism on both sides referred to the longer poems. In the shorter there is much in common: neither in the *Ode to Autumn*, for example, nor in the *Ode to the West Wind* can anybody doubt the maturity or richness of the ore.

During 1817, Shelley's last year in England, the relationship became no closer but was in many ways an exemplary one, full of courtesy and frank recognition of differences. Criticism involved no jealousy but proceeded in each from a concern for the other's fame. Keats instructed his publisher to send copies of his poems to Shelley as soon as they appeared, and Shelley returned the compliment and the token of good-will.

In March 1818 Shelley left England for Italy seeking health and sun and flying from the shadows still cast by his first marriage. Italy was to give him life and colour and warmth: "I depend on these things for life, for in the smoke of cities and the tumult of human kind, and the chilling fogs and rains of our own country I can hardly be said to live."

Man and poet indeed depended on these things. In Italy he was to sing as never before, and Italy was to pass into his song. Few can visit that lovely land without an aching sense of frustration. All things are there to stir the mind and the least imaginative of us are possessed by the desire to absorb, to transmute and to create. For an Englishman in Italy to have read Shelley is to think of Shelley who, most of all Englishmen perhaps save one, had the quality which Italy demands.

Many have related the Shelleys' wanderings in those early Italian years. Passing through the Alpine valleys by way of France and Switzerland they moved about Piedmont, Tuscany and the northern regions, finding fresh beauties everywhere. Paintings and churches, sun and sky and lake fill Shelley's letters of the period. Happiness and freedom found their outlet in verse. Meanwhile, unlike many Englishmen in Italy, Shelley became no selfish æsthete, no fugitive into inner worlds of sensation. The affairs of mankind continued to occupy the philanthropist and, as ever, he was busied with the troubles of his friends. Among the many who turned to him in their perplexity was Byron, that other exile the aroma of whose escapades in Venice still faintly pursues his countrymen in the Venetian mind. Then there were Shelley's own troubles; the children of his first marriage taken from him by the Lord Chancellor, and an infant daughter carried away by a mysterious illness at Este. In verse appeared his sorrow too Mirrored in the *Stanzas written in the Euganean Hills*, those easy flowing lines where, hardly less than Canaletto or Guardi, he has caught the glow and twinkle of the City of the Doges, we find something more than pure objective beauty. Out of the vast of waters rose images of his own unhappiness and he hints a longing for Pindar's "Blessed Isles":

> "Many a green isle needs must be
> In the deep wide sea of Misery,
> Or the mariner, worn and wan,
> Never thus could voyage on. . . ."

Sixty years later Carducci, standing by Shelley's grave in Rome, imagined the reception in those islands of the "Titan spirit in a virgin's form", led thither by Sophocles emerging with him as guide from the realms of the Sea-goddess.[1]

It was in November 1818 that Shelley first saw and was enchanted by the plot amid cypresses and oleanders where lay the non-Catholic foreigners who had died in Rome. He and Mary stayed a week, visited the Colosseum or the Forum every day and drank deep of antiquity.

There followed several months in Naples, Vesuvius, Pompeii; the joy of boating, sunsets over Capri and Ischia, the merriment of song and *festa* were not wasted. But again he was miserable, tormented first by illness and then by the complications of a slander resulting from one of his usual pieces of ingenuous philanthropy. The "dejection" felt amid such beauty produced the wonderful Naples stanzas:

[1] See p. 38.

28

"The sun is warm, the sky is clear,
  The waves are dancing fast and bright,
  Blue isles and snowy mountains wear
  The purple noon's transparent might. . . ."

Despair itself grew mild in the blue reflections and so might death
be. He longed to sleep

"Till death like sleep might steal on me,
  And I might feel in the warm air
  My cheek grow cold, and hear the sea
  Breathe o'er my dying brain its last monotony."

There are many places in the writings both of Keats and of
Shelley where the prescience might seem remarkable, and yet, so
strong is our own sense of a pattern pervading their lives, that it
seems hardly remarkable at all.

In March 1819 began a three-months' stay in Rome. Shelley
joined in *feste* and *funzioni* with a joy marred only by the reformer's
disgust at intermittent examples of Papal tyranny, and for the first
time felt a liking for the Italian people. Meanwhile he saturated
his mind with antiquity. Inspiration and energy were at their
height and to the happiness and leisure afforded by Rome we owe
much of his finest work, not least the greater part of *Prometheus
Unbound*. This he called "my best poem" and in it man and artist
gave to the world an expression of the spirit of humanity touched
with that Spirit of Delight which—too rare a visitor, as Shelley
complained—could find its recollection in the tranquility of the
Baths of Caracalla. These ruins became a little kingdom for him.

But sorrow came, this time with overwhelming suddenness.
The three-year-old William Shelley, delight of his parents, fell ill
and died like his sister. Overtones of this sorrow and of the child's
burial near the pyramid of Cestius were to sound later in the
elegy on Keats. The Shelleys left Rome which had become
intolerable.

The next few years saw the completion of *The Cenci* and
produced among other longer poems *The Witch of Atlas*,
The Sensitive Plant, *The Mask of Anarchy* and *Epipsychidion*

Meanwhile cloud, moon, and skylark, and all the poet felt and saw found their way into immortal lyrics. Moving about North Italy the Shelleys lived in various places and grew specially fond of Pisa. Perhaps to these years we owe something of the elastic movement and round-syllabled music of the Shelley line, for the poet was reading Ariosto amid the heard harmonies of that Tuscan speech wherein even Manzoni sought perfection. But we owe to them, above all, the leisure and the liberty wherein Shelley's inspiration could work. In Italy, for all the shadows, he felt unchained like his own *Prometheus*, and escaping at last into a freedom wherein he could build his metaphysical systems, could escape thence again, like his skylark, to pour forth the lovely lyrics "in profuse strains of unpremeditated art".

For Keats too, the years 1818–19 had been great years. The brilliant youth had evolved, with astonishing rapidity, into the mature man; and the poet of *Endymion* published in April 1818, one month after Shelley's departure from England, was now the poet of *Hyperion, Lamia, The Eve of St. Agnes, La Belle Dame Sans Merci* and the great odes and sonnets. Herein, learned or divinely realized, the power of Greek imagination, and the magic of the earlier Italian Renaissance, had met the very genius of English poetry. The marriage and departure of one brother, the death in consumption of the other, travel, study and creation, had filled a period of activity to which he brought an "intensity" all his own. From his letters, meanwhile, there emerges a genius for friendship and a wisdom for life and living hardly to be paralleled in any man of twenty-three or four. The void in his life caused by the loss of his brothers was filled for a while by his friends, notably by Charles Brown with whom he "domesticated" at Hampstead. But his nature required a deeper stimulus, both intellectually and emotionally, and this he found in his love for Fanny Brawne. They were engaged on Christmas Day 1818 and it was in the following spring that love and genius grew into full flower. Then came disaster. In December 1819 with the return of the sore throat which had long been an intermittent trouble his health began to fail. In February 1820, during an attack of coughing, he saw his own death-warrant. Keats was a qualified medical man. "I know the colour of that blood. It's arterial blood: I must die." For the rest of that winter and through the summer he was an invalid, nursed in turn by Brown, by the Hunts, and by the Brawnes. In July 1820 appeared the great little volume containing *Lamia*, etc. Within a month he was an established poet. Within another month it had become clear that an English winter would kill him and he was ordered by his doctors to Italy.

Shelley, as we have seen, was no whole-hearted admirer of Keats' every line of verse. Nevertheless in August 1819 we find him remarking on the promise of *Endymion* and in May 1820 he wrote to his publisher that Keats was going to show himself a great poet—"like the sun to burst through the clouds". He allowed no detail of Keats' personal or literary interests to escape him and he was, in the meantime, battling with Byron's inability to see in his friend anything more than a "Cockney idol". "Blackwood's attacks on *Endymion* and the attacks in the *Quarterly* had drawn Shelley closer than anything to Keats. Ever ready to break a lance with authority where freedom of thought was concerned he saw in these and other attacks yet another manifestation (and one tinged with religious prejudices) in favour of the ruling classes. Then he heard that Keats was under sentence of death from the doctors. Immediately he wrote him a letter, slightly formal but perfect in its way and characteristic of Shelley the Helper-in-Trouble.

"Mrs. Shelley unites with myself in urging the request that you would take up your residence with us. . . . You ought at all events to see Italy, and your health which I suggest as a motive, might be an excuse to you. I spare declamation about the statues and the paintings and the ruins—and what is a greater piece of forbearance—about the mountains the streams and the fields, the colours of the sky, and the sky itself —"

Keats replied with gratitude, if ambiguously, and spoke warmly to Charles Brown of Shelley's invitation. As yet he was uncertain of his plans but he proposed to spend the winter in Rome and would, he hoped, see the Shelleys in the spring.

On 13th September, 1820 Keats left Hampstead for ever and

"with the sensation of a soldier marching up to a Battery" faced the journey to Italy. Accompanied by his artist friend Severn, who risked much for his sake, he embarked a few days later on the brig *Maria Crowther* and on 21st October, after a long and painful voyage, reached Naples.

On 11th November Shelley was inquiring Keats' whereabouts from Mrs. Hunt:

"I am anxiously expecting him in Italy, when I shall take care to bestow every possible attention on him. I consider his a most valuable life, and I am deeply interested in his safety. I intend to be the physician both of his body and his soul, to keep the one warm, and to teach the other Greek and Spanish. I am aware indeed, in part, that I am nourishing a rival who will far surpass me; and this is an additional motive, and will be an added pleasure."

While at Naples Keats received another offer of hospitality from Shelley. But the plans were by then made for proceeding to Rome.

Of Keats' last months of life and of his sufferings the faithful Severn has left us full accounts. From Keats' own letters—the one to Brown written while the *Maria Crowther* lay off Yarmouth and the few final ones from Italy—the central cause of that suffering is plain. "I can bear to die—I cannot bear to leave her. O God! God! God! Everything I have in my trunks that reminds me of her goes through me like a spear. . . . Land and Sea, weakness and decline are great separators, but death is the great divorcer for ever."

The life was spent which had blazed into full flame in the spring of 1819 with his love for Fanny Brawne. Spent too was the flame of poetry. For some days Keats and Severn lay off Naples enduring the uncomfortable rigours of quarantine. Before them the smoke of Vesuvius curled above the unsurpassable blue beauty of the Bay and, there, in the land of the Sirens and of the Sibyl, opened all around them that world of antiquity and poetical suggestion at which Shelley's letter had hinted. But the Keats who earlier had caught in his letters and verse so much of the scenery

SHELLEY'S HOUSE AT LERICI
from a water-colour painting in Keats House, Hampstead.
(by permission of the Hampstead Corporation)

THE PROTESTANT CEMETERY, ROME
(above) graves of Keats and Severn
(below) grave of Shelley

and romance of England and Scotland was now "no longer a citizen of the world". "I cannot", he writes to Brown, "say a word about Naples; I do not feel at all concerned in the thousand novelties around me."

It was more than ill-health and discomfort which had killed the poetry. Imagination was not dead but it was elsewhere: "I dare not fix my mind upon Fanny . . . my imagination is horribly vivid about her."

The friends went ashore and the fairyland vanished in the noise, dirt and smells by which they were "quite taken aback" and against which the old humanity and humour of the sick man was not now proof: equally distressing to the Liberal were the ever-present examples of the tyranny of King Ferdinand. Of the two routes to Rome—both to be of bloody memory to a generation taught by a later dictator to use its "monstrous armies"—they took the coastal one. Thus they did not pass under the grim hill surmounted by an abbey whose monks were one day to guard their relics from the barbarian. Passing through Terracina they crossed the Campagna, which Keats likened to "an inland sea", and entered the Lateran Gate of Rome on 17th November, 1820.

Keats had just three months to live. Till 10th December his health was moderately good and walks and rides were possible. On that day he had a relapse and after weeks of horrible suffering he died on 23rd February, 1821, tended by Severn and by Dr. Clark, the Scottish doctor to whom an introduction had been arranged in London. The details of this "posthumous life", as Keats called it, are recorded by Severn and by the biographers. Rome holds the rest.

Dr. Clark, whose professional career is open to criticism which must be viewed in the light of the knowledge of his day, went far in personal kindness to Keats and Severn and it was he who found them the lodgings close to his own in the Piazza di Spagna.

This very characteristic square still preserves most of its seventeenth and eighteenth century features and has altered little in a century and a quarter. The orange-russet houses catch the Roman light as they did in Keats' time and in the centre Bernini's *Barcaccia*, a fountain constructed in 1627 in the form of a galley, still marks the site of an arena where real galleys once fought bloody naval battles to amuse the deified Domitian. But of an unforgettable picture it is neither the houses nor the fountain which stands out most in the memory of a traveller. Down from an upper terrace leading to the Pincio Gardens sweeps the magnificent eighteenth-century Scalinata of Alessandro Specchi, a vast cataract of steps which, winding across and round a series of transversal terraces, pours into the square as if it would swamp the galley. Above, on the topmost terrace and balancing the fountain below, stands an ancient obelisk and, behind it, the twin towers and well-proportioned façade of Santa Trinita dei Monti complete a bold and satisfying perspective by which the square is entirely dominated. As we move behind the fountain, to the left or to the right, the perspective moves too, and the change and flow of line and curve complete the impression of a cataract to which the fountain supplies the sound.

No. 26, Piazza di Spagna, preserved to-day by the Keats-Shelley Memorial, lies at the foot of the steps and we see it on the right as we approach them from the fountain. If Keats' life, as has often been remarked, was no less "an Allegory" than Shakespeare's, and if his works, like Shakespeare's, are its commentary, it may likewise be said that the places where he lived and died form inspired and fitting marginalia. Like his home in Hampstead those last lodgings in Rome have an air of inevitability and seem a part of his destiny. In the two cool rooms, high-ceilinged though not large, he could find quiet without gloom and, while removed from the bustle of that world of which he was "no longer a citizen", he could look out upon a "window world" of colour and of life. The larger of the rooms faces upon the busy square and the smaller upon the steps. These, in his day, were a noted hiring ground for artists' models. The poet's eye must have found pleasure when it could in the variously garbed throng of professional saints, brigands and Virgin Mothers, and since no Italian crowd ever fails in appreciation of a theatrical gesture, especially when executed by an Englishman, they in their turn must have richly enjoyed the incident, related by Severn, of Keats' defenestration of his dinner. Below bubbled the fountain and from the church above came the singing of the French nuns for whom the delighted Mendelssohn later composed a chant.

In Keats' day, that heyday of Papal dictatorship, the Piazza di Spagna was the centre of the foreigners' quarter in Rome.[1] Behind it lie the Pincio Gardens. Straight across the square from Keats' window the long Via Condotti, renowned for its jewellers and then gay with confetti at carnival-time, leads towards the Tiber. Turning to the right across the square from No. 26 we soon reach the Piazza del Popolo and the gate which was once the City's northern limit. Through this gate the Roman legions once swept north to conquer and to build; this way in 1944 fled the beaten legions of th' latest barbarian invader, and this way, on a Sunday morning in Keats' time, streamed the tiny pageant of liberty formed by the proud Protestant families with their children their nursemaids and their prayer-books, going to worship without the walls.

From the Piazza di Spagna the ordinary nineteenth century tourist could radiate in all directions to that vast outer world of Rome which is "the heart of Europe and the chronicle of Man's long march to civilization". For Keats this outer world was unattainable, still more so the distant height of Janiculum whence our historian looked down. Closer to the Piazza di Spagna lay another place, itself of rest and beauty, from which he could survey the Promised Land.

To-day from the Keats-Shelley Memorial House we may follow his footsteps up the Scalinata into those gardens with which among the "score of civilizations" the French genius has enriched Rome. Here on the Pincio once stood the villa where Lucullus feasted Cicero and Pompey and where Messalina revelled with her lovers and was murdered; here in the nineteenth century was the fashionable rendezvous "bright with sunset and pink parasols" where Keats found air and warmth and such intolerable reminders. We may look eastwards to the Borghese Gardens and north-eastwards towards Soracte and the other heights which enfold so much history. Then we turn westwards and across the terraces, leaning on the balustrade, look out across the Piazza del Popolo, to the sea of churches, palaces and ruins, to St. Peter's, Monte Mario and the Janiculum standing out beyond the Tiber against the sky, and to the Campagna reaching towards the sea. Below us,

[1] Byron had lodged in the Piazza di Spagna and Shelley in the Corso, not far away.

bathed in that Roman light for which there are no words, lies the Eternal City. Like Shelley let us "spare declamation". As we look down we feel, here too, "the presence of all the centuries of European civilization" and are dazed by the reality of things written and read. Nor is it difficult to feel something of the presence of Keats. We think of Shelley's fulfilment in Italy and of his own unfulfilment and, as a score of familiar lines packed with their too prescient imagery go ringing through the mind, we hear again that despairing cry and know what a thing it was for himself and for us that he stood in Rome with "an intellect in splints".

> "The feel of not to feel it,
> When there is none to heal it
> Nor numbéd sense to steel it,
> Was never said in rhyme."

So died Keats on 23rd February, 1821, desiring to have written above him in the Protestant Cemetery, "Here lies one whose name was writ in water". Severn, who now lies beside him, set up the words in stone, adding above them the symbol—and the summary—of a broken lyre.

It was April before the news reached Shelley at Pisa. Deeply moved by personal sorrow he was concerned, as well, for Keats' fame and at once wrote to Severn discussing a memoir and enquiring about the fate of unpublished poems. By June *Adonais*, the immortal elegy into which he poured his feelings, had received a final form. Never before had Shelley displayed such anxiety that a poem of his should find a large and enthusiastic audience. It was more than a memorial to Keats: it was a frontal attack by Shelley-the-Liberator on the citadel of Prejudice represented by the reviewers whom he believed to have hastened Keats' death. In the preface is arraigned "the foremost of these literary prostitutes".

"Miserable man! You, one of the meanest, have wantonly defiled one of the noblest specimens of the workmanship of God. Nor shall it be your excuse, that, murderer as you are, you have spoken daggers but used none."

The personal feeling was real:

> "Alas! that all we loved of him should be
> But for our grief as if it had not been,
> And grief itself be mortal."

Here is something beyond a mere exercise in the manner of Bion and Moschus; few lines, anywhere, penetrate more sensitively into the pathology of the moods which follow loss.

But into *Adonais* Shelley poured more than an expression of his own sorrow and a valiant defence of the dead poet. With these things were interfused a sense of, as it were, some dark Aeschylean destiny linking himself to Keats and both to Rome. "Go thou to Rome" he tells the mourner—

> "Go thou to Rome,—at once the Paradise,
> The grave, the city and the wilderness;
> And where its wrecks like shattered mountains rise,
> And flowering weeds and fragrant copses dress
> The bones of Desolation's nakedness
> Pass, till the spirit of the spot shall lead
> Thy footsteps to a slope of green access
> Where, like an infant's smile, over the dead
> A light of laughing flowers along the grass is shed."

The reference to Shelley's lost child needs no underlining. With a sense of a dark destiny went the foreboding, now hardly dark at all, of his own end. In *Alastor*, in the Naples Stanzas, and elsewhere this had been already shown, but in *Adonais* the conviction rises to a climax.

> "The breath whose might I have invoked in song
> Descends on me: my spirit's bark is driven
> Far from the shore, far from the trembling throng
> Whose sails were never to the tempest given;
> The massy earth and spheréd skies are riven!
> I am born darkly, fearfully, afar;
> Whilst burning through the inmost veil of Heaven,
> The soul of Adonais, like a star,
> Beacons from the abode where the Eternal are."

37

And to the same climax rises that sense of the inevitable which follows many of us through the pages of Keats and Shelley and through their paths in Italy.

Shelley himself had just another year to live. The summer of 1822 found him at Lerici on the Tuscan coast surrounded by congenial friends and as happy with nautical as with metaphysical experiments. Into his last and unfinished poem, *The Triumph of Life*, went much of the thought and feeling of the year; the poem shows signs of a mental poise he had not hitherto attained but its final resolution we shall never know. Byron had moved to Pisa and continued to attract and to trouble his better angel. Meanwhile Shelley was busy with a scheme for bringing to Italy Leigh Hunt and his numerous family and for starting him, with Byron's help, on a literary venture in the Liberal cause.

On 1st July, 1822 the two old friends met at Leghorn. They spent some days together and explored the beauties of Pisa, where the Hunts took up their residence with Byron. On 8th July, accompanied by a sailor boy, Shelley and his friend Williams were at Leghorn, impatient to return to their wives at Lerici. Against the advice of more experienced mariners, who foresaw a storm, they set sail in Shelley's little boat the *Don Juan*. The *Don Juan* was last seen ten miles out from Viareggio vanishing into haze. That haze has never lifted.

It was 18th July before Trelawny, Shelley's adventurer friend who led the anxious searchers, heard that two bodies had been washed up on the shore. One, found near Viareggio, was Shelley's. It still bore the jacket "with a volume of Sophocles[1] in one pocket and Keats' poems in the other, doubled back as if the reader, in the act of reading, had hastily thrust it away". The other, four miles away, was Williams'. The sailor-boy was found later.

In the Hampstead days Shelley had been fond of prefacing his flights of humorous fancy with the lines from *Richard II:*

> "For God's sake, let us sit upon the ground
> And tell sad stories of the deaths of Kings."

In a reference to this Keats had added, "Tell him that there are

[1] See p. 28.

strange stories of the death of Poets". The succeeding episode, stranger still, is equally a part of the Shelley pattern.

Mary and Shelley's friends were determined that he should be buried in Rome, as he would have wished, near Keats and his son William. But the Italian quarantine laws which had afflicted Keats living now stood in the path of Shelley dead. Trelawny, backed by British official influence in Florence, finally induced the authorities to allow the proceeding provided that they performed previously "the ancient custom of burning and reducing the body to ashes". On 18th August, 1822 the ceremony took place, with every detail that could have been conceived by Homer, Virgil—or Shelley.

A pyre was built on the shore near Viareggio under the direction of Trelawny and, while the hastily-made grave in the sand was being disinterred, Byron and Leigh Hunt arrived in a carriage. With them came the Health Officer. Thus fittingly represented at Shelley's exequies stood not only the world of poetry of thought and of virile energy personified in his three friends but also the sullen world of official tyranny. Trelawny describes the setting:

"The lonely and grand scenery that surrounded us so exactly harmonized with Shelley's genius that I could imagine his spirit soaring over us. The sea with the islands of Gorgona, Capraia and Elba was before us; old battlemented watchtowers stretched along the coast, backed by the marble-crested Apennines glistening in the sun, picturesque in their diversified outlines, and not a human dwelling was in sight."

Frankincense and salt were offered up and "more wine was poured over Shelley's dead body than he had consumed during his life". Nor was verse wanting in the heroic tale: Keats' last poems found in his dead friend's pocket were cast into the flames. So, in that final beacon, *Adonais* had his part. On the picture of Byron swimming out to sea from the intolerable strange and splendid scene the curtain drops. What thoughts went surging through that fevered mind we may not know; perhaps the omnipresent spirit of Shelley, in his turn made one with Nature, was beaconing him to a new sense of his birthright, perhaps already in the cleansing waters were born redemption and a hero's death in Greece.

In Byron's last and Shelleyan adventure Trelawny played his part. Like Severn he survived to a ripe old age and men and women yet alive may have seen the scarred hand that drew a poet's heart from the burning. Fittingly he now lies in the Protestant Cemetery in Rome beside those ashes over which he had set the inspired quotation:

> "Nothing of him that doth fade
> But doth suffer a sea-change
> Into something rich and strange"

Less imaginative people than Carducci and d'Annunzio have remarked the strange sense that is felt amid the cypresses and the Roman light of the presence of Keats and Shelley. It was not for nothing that the paths which met in Hampstead led to Rome and that Shelley, drawn to Keats in life, was linked to him by destiny in death.

> "'Tis Adonais calls! Oh, hasten thither,
> No more let Life divide what Death can join together"

Nowhere, perhaps, more nearly than in Rome can we feel the measure of their magnitude. The universal setting which seems to dwarf a transient generation and its systems does not dwarf Keats and Shelley: they are a part of it:

> ".... Rome's azure sky,
> Flowers, ruins, statues, music, words, are weak
> The glory they transfuse with fitting truth to speak."

NEVILLE ROGERS.

THE PROTESTANT CEMETERY

ROME 1889

"THE cemetery was deserted save for a few gardeners who were watering the plants under the wall, swinging their cans with a steady level movement, in silence. Into the sky rose the perpendicular lines of the cypresses, all but motionless, their tips alone quivering in the sun's last rays. Between the smooth straight trunks with their greenish hue like Tibur stone appeared the white tombs and the square slabs, the broken columns, the vaults, the urns. Out of the darkening clumps a dark mystery, a religious calm, something, as it were, of the very sweetness of humanity issued like a clear cool streamlet from a rock. That unbroken symmetry of tree-shapes, that unadorned whiteness of monumental masonry brought a sense of deep and restful peace into the mind. . . . Between the trees and over the tombs red-clustering oleander swayed gracefully while at every breath of wind rose bushes dropped their petals on the grass. . . . Now and then the silence was broken by the cry of some wandering bird.

Between the low myrtle-bushes they reached the graves of Shelley and Trelawny. The jessamine climbing over the ancient ruin was in flower but of the violets only thick growing leaves remained. From here the cypress-tips were level with the eye-line and they glowed still brighter in the sun now sinking behind Monte Testaccio. Aloft, towards the Aventine swam a violet cloud rimmed with burning gold. . . .

They walked on to find the grave of John Keats, the poet of *Endymion*. . . . Now an evening breeze was getting up and the sky behind the hill was crossed with glowing bars amid which cloud upon cloud was melting, consumed as in a funeral pyre. Erect against a field of light the cypress-ranks grew in grandeur and mystery, pierced through and through with shafts of light, their tips all quivering. The statue of Psyche at the end of the central pathway had taken on a pale flesh-like tint. The oleanders beyond had become a moving dome of darkest red. Over Cestius'

41

pyramid rose a sickle moon across a sky green as the sea and deep as the waters of a still bay. . . .

They went down the central pathway to the gate. The gardeners were still watering the plants under the wall, swinging their cans with a steady level movement, in silence."

GABRIELE D'ANNUNZIO.
(From *Il Piacere* 1889: tr. N.R.)

ON THE FAME OF JOHN KEATS

1947

I think I shall be among the English Poets after my death.
(Keats, October 1818.)

> Hobbs hints blue—straight he turtle eats:
> Nobbs prints blue—claret crowns his cup:
> Nokes outdares Stokes in azure feats,—
> Both gorge. Who fished the murex up?
> What porridge had John Keats?
>
> (Popularity, Robert Browning, c.1850.)

If one English poet might be recalled to-day from the dead to continue the work which he left unfinished on earth, it is probable the crown of his country's desire would be set on the head of John Keats.

(Robert Bridges, 1895.)

. . . his greatest poetry was, as he wished it to be, a spontaneous utterance of the complete being, and for that reason is the only English poetry that is truly like Shakespeare's. . . .

Keats was the poet-prophet. He was one of those who initiated men into the worship of the thing that is; who fought, thus positively, against the worship of the thing that is not.

(J. Middleton Murry, 1924 and 1932.)

IN 1829, when Brown broached the subject of a biography to her, Fanny Brawne wrote of her lover, "I fear the kindest act would be to let him rest forever in the obscurity to which unhappy circumstances have condemned him." Influenced perhaps by that sad epitaph of Keats' own devising Fanny exaggerated the world's neglect. As poet Keats already had enough reputation to warrant in that very year the issue of a

Galignani edition[1] in Paris, and as man a certain notoriety; a notoriety fostered by the preface to *Adonais*, in its turn brought to public notice by Shelley's violent death at sea and by the fashionable Byron's comment in *Don Juan*:

> John Keats, who was killed by one critique,
> Just as he really promised something great,
> If not intelligible, without Greek,
> Contrived to talk about the gods of late,
> Much as they might have been supposed to speak.
> Poor fellow! his was an untoward fate;
> 'Tis strange the mind, that very fiery particle,
> Should let itself be snuffed out by an article.

Shelley had rendered great homage to his friend, but homage to some extent mistaken and misleading. Though affected during his last days in England by the poisonous attacks in *Blackwood's* and the *Quarterly*, attacks persisted in by "the Mother of Mischief" even when he was known to be seriously ill, Keats was not "snuffed out by an article", nor was he a willowy aesthete

> . . . who grew,
> Like a pale flower by some sad maiden cherished,
> And fed with true-love tears, instead of dew. . . .

Keats in health was a man robust in mind and spirit. The basil of his poetry might feed itself on grief and suffering but it grew green and vigorous. Fostered by *Adonais* and by Byron's verse the legend of Keats' death at the hands of the reviewers (kept up by some Liberal writers as a convenient stick with which to whack the Tory critics) persisted for many years and was in Rome crystallized in a phrase common among shallow-pated tourists who, guffawing over the tragic epitaph, would exclaim, "And his works in milk-and-water!" But though a generation still dominated by the more rudely muscular rime of Lord Byron repeated

[1] As a pirated edition it could not be circulated here but was sold and reprinted in America—where in consequence Keats' fame grew more rapidly. For an amplification of this see *Keats' Reputation in America to 1848*, Hyder E. Rollins, The Harvard University Press, or Geoffrey Cumberlege.

this parrot-phrase in depreciation of the poet (often, Severn remarked, not having read him) men and women were already visiting that grave in the Protestant Cemetery. As the legend of Keats grew its combined foundation of hostility and interest begot another, that Keats was an effeminate writer only fit for the ladies; in the words of the unpoetic Carlyle, full of "weak-eyed maudlin sensibility".

But beneath this superficial notoriety a ferment was at work. Beyond the immediate circle of Keats' devoted friends a few finer spirits of the age were reading, studying and praising John Keats. Walter Savage Landor paid early homage, in 1828 heralding, or perhaps inspiring a more widely known dictum of Matthew Arnold's some forty years later with "in none of our poets, with the sole exception of Shakespeare, do we find so many phrases so happy in their boldness."

The first poet to be influenced by Keats, drawing so direct an inspiration that he might be called disciple, was Thomas Hood whose *The Plea of the Midsummer Fairies* (1827) is in part a loving corollary of his master with themes closely akin, titles in direct imitation and unmistakable Keatsian echoes. One poem, *Ruth*, actually begins with the line "She stood breast high amid the corn". But Hood, as brother-in-law to Reynolds, Keats' friend, and having easy access to work published and unpublished, might be considered one of the Keatsian circle. Certainly *The Plea of the Midsummer Fairies* hardly went beyond that circle: the edition languished upon Longmans' shelves until Hood himself bought it up "to save it from the butter shops". The voice of an authentic serious poet was, to the loss of literature, drowned by the louder tones of Hood the already established writer of comic verse.

Keats' original volumes, now so precious in hard money, might for many years be picked up out of the fourpenny boxes of second-hand booksellers; but since there were eager sensitive fingers to probe for treasure perhaps this apparent neglect had a part in the growth of his fame. A fourpenny box is more easy of access than a bookseller's shelf or the wrapping of a pat of butter. By the 'thirties the devoted work of Dilke and Hunt in keeping green the memory of their friend was showing fruit.

Keats had become a cult with the "Apostles", that group of Cambridge undergraduates including Arthur Hallam, Richard Monckton Milnes and, most significantly, Alfred Tennyson. For Tennyson, Keats always remained first among the Romantics; "greater than them all—Wordsworth, Coleridge, Byron, Shelley, every one of 'em—is Keats, who died at twenty-five—thousands of faults! . . . but he's wonderful!"

Tennyson, though his heir, was, paradoxically, Keats' forerunner in the 'forties. His mediævalism, clothed in easy mellifluous verse and conveyed in vivid coloured pictures, paved the way for a wider reception of Keats' verbal magic, for the richly-dyed world of romance of *St. Agnes' Eve*. Mariana and The Lady of Shalott were a social introduction in Victorian drawing-rooms for fair Isabel and Madeline "asleep in lap of legends old".

In January, 1835, after Richard Woodhouse's collection of Keatsiana, including unpublished work, came to him by inheritance, John Taylor wrote, "I should like to print a complete Edition of Keats' Poems, with several of his letters, but the world cares nothing for him—I fear that even 250 copies would not sell". But six years later William Smith Williams of Fleet Street thought it worth while to put out the contents of the three volumes of 1817, 1818 and 1820 in a popular form, and in 1842 a decorative edition with Hilton's portrait of Keats as frontispiece; thus furthering a demand for the Life so long awaited by those who had loved the poet.

With the publication in 1848 of Monckton Milnes' *Life, Letters and Literary Remains* Keats came into his own not only as poet, a finely dowered poet of the senses, but as man. One might know him now as he was, as he walked and talked. Further to enhance his fame a new order of poets had arisen, conscious devotees who were more deeply to underline the accepted qualities of Keats, men who claimed a world of richness and colour as their heritage. Though Rossetti and his peers might hint blue, print blue, employing with an art less subtle the splendid Tyrian dye, product of that mollusc, the murex, which Browning so dramatically and happily pictured Keats as fishing up, they bred a class of readers with an ear sensitively attuned to verbal beauty, an eye cleared for light and colour. Taylor and Hessey, those generous far-sighted publishers, sowed for Moxon to reap; Keats' poems "priced and saleable at last" went into edition after edition. Severn, returning to Rome as British Consul in 1861, wrote rejoicing of Keats' fame:

> "not as manifested by new editions of his works, or by the contests of publishers about him, or by the way in which most new works are illustrated with quotations from him, or by the fact that some favourite lines of his have passed into proverbs, but by the touching evidence of his *silent grave*. That grave which I can remember as once the object of ridicule, has now become the poetic shrine of the world's pilgrims who care and strive to live in the happy and imaginative region of poetry. The head-stone, having twice sunk, owing to its faulty foundation, has been twice renewed by loving strangers, and each time, as I am informed, these strangers were Americans. Here they do not strew flowers—as was the wont of olden times, but they pluck everything that is green and living on the grave of the poet. The custodian tells me, that notwithstanding all his pains in sowing and planting he cannot 'meet the great consumption. . . .' When the *Custode* complained to me of the continued thefts, and asked what he was to do, I replied, 'Sow and plant twice as much; extend the poet's domain; for, as it was so scanty during his short life, surely it ought to be yielded to him two-fold in his grave."

Men were beginning to think of Keats as a man of rare quality: *Hyperion* was no longer regarded as a grand Miltonic exercise. With a knowledge of Keats' life, his thought and development, the early lusher work was falling into place as prelude to a high destiny in part fulfilled in the 1820 volume. In the 'eighties by loving interpretation and careful scholarship Harry Buxton Forman brought both poems and letters more richly before a generation attuned to Keats: Sidney Colvin wrote a new Life in the series *English Men of Letters*. By the end of the century Keats was not only secure in poetic fame but recognized as a thinker; though it was left to our own time to know his ultimate greatness as man and philosopher. The debt in profound criticism, in spreading a knowledge of Keats, to Λ. C. Bradley, Dr. Bridges, Dr. de Sélincourt and Professor H. W. Garrod; to Amy Lowell, Mr. Maurice Buxton Forman, Mr. Edmund Blunden and Mr. J. Middleton Murry needs no emphasis of mine. To Mr. Middleton Murry has fallen the privilege of interpreting the spiritual quality of John Keats the poet-prophet "straining after particles of light in the midst of a great darkness", and in the midst of woe attaining to "the supreme of power", "The top of sovereignty".

DOROTHY HEWLETT.

Note. In the writing of this article I am more than a little indebted to that excellent book *Keats and the Victorians*, George H. Ford, Humphrey Milford, The Oxford University Press.

D.H.

LIFE MASK OF JOHN KEATS
by BENJAMIN ROBERT HAYDON
Reproduced by permission of the London Borough of Camden
from the collection at Keats House, Hampstead.

KEATS ON HIS DEATH-BED

JOSEPH SEVERN

The original in the Keats-Shelley Memorial House, Rome, bears Severn's inscription: "3 o'clock Mg. drawn to keep me awake—a deadly sweat was on him all this night."

ON THE DRAWING DEPICTING
JOHN KEATS IN DEATH[1]

Now, from afar, to the stilled Singer's head there
Reach the horizon-distances unending,
And agony falls again, past comprehending,
On the dark form, an agony that bred there.

So things remain; the drawing's caught—by mourning
Quickened, you'd say: a second-brief creation—
The flickering passage of a pity scorning
The very facts of Being and Cessation.

Whose is that face? No more the mind's endeavour
Can features speak with mind together-clinging!
O eye that will no more Beauty be wringing[2]
Out of some Truth-in-Things, unhidden never!—
O gate of singing,
Young mouth, surrendered now, closed now, alas, for ever!—

Only the forehead seems to be achieving
A lasting bridge across the dissolution,—
To the tired, tumbling lock's irresolution
A mild reproach, full of most gentle grieving.

RAINER MARIA RILKE
translated by Neville Rogers

---

[1] Written early in 1914 and suggested by Joseph Severn's drawing—Rilke being under the impression that Keats was actually dead when it was made.

[2] Should my version of lines 11–14 seem over-interpretative, an alternative rendering, closer to the words of the passage, if not to the purport of the poem, might be

> From things of life, now life's declined for ever,
> O eye that will no more Beauty be wringing
> O gate of singing,
> Young mouth surrendered now, alas, to open never!

THE FAME OF SHELLEY

1947

"MR PERCY BYSSHE SHELLEY—but we will not trust ourselves with this person; Tacitus has taught us, that there are some offences so flagitious in their nature, that it is necessary, for the benefit of public morals, to conceal their punishment; we leave them, therefore, to the silent vengeance which vice sooner or later *must* wreak upon itself. Mr. John Keats is, we hope, of another class."

This passage, one of a great many in the same style, appeared in *The British Critic* for July, 1818; the occasion was the reviewing of Leigh Hunt's book of poems, *Foliage*, in which as in one place after another that author had a word to say in assurance and in promotion of the fame of Keats and Shelley. It was the time when the political adversaries of Hunt and his fellow reformists were most determined that none of them should achieve fame or anything else. The story of the campaign against them all, evidenced in a multitude of printed detestations and calumnies mingled no doubt with a proportion of fair criticism, is not a new one. It might yet be written in much greater detail than it has yet received, though scholarly hands have produced parts of it with accuracy; but ample volumes would be needed for such a survey. In this miscellany a glance at characteristic signs of the progress of the fame of Shelley in particular is all that can be indulged.

Shelley in the south was still receiving attentions from such as *The British Critic* when it came his way to utter some words on his own account concerning his fame. So far as personal reputation goes, he was not very different from the rest of men; he had no desire to incur infamy, with its inconveniences, and he could enjoy recognition and the favour of the day. But, feeling that his ideals were those which could and must lead to the betterment of society, he perceived that his writings needed the prospering gale of public excitement. Poems or tractates, *those* must become famous. One day when the woodland near Florence began to be astir with the wind of autumn, Shelley wrote that Ode which at

length becomes a petition to the active spirit abroad in that
energy:

> "Drive my dead thoughts over the universe
> Like withered leaves to quicken a new birth!
> And by the incantation of this verse,
> Scatter, as from an unextinguished hearth
> Ashes and sparks, my words among mankind!"

In truth that dissemination, poetical and philosophical, had
already begun. Some imperfections necessarily occurred as the
genius of Shelley made its way; he was not in his later years among
the warmest friends of his early essay in verse *Queen Mab*, and
yet that work was the one with which his name was generally
associated. Those who would destroy him referred to its irreligion,
and those who were discontented with the state of things looked
for it and, if they could find it, exulted in its strength. It was hard
to get; copies were sold at high prices, manuscript copies were
made; and when in 1821 an astute and needy bookseller printed a
pirate edition he found plenty of buyers. All this was half a joke,
half a misery to the author, who had been long conscious that the
youth of his bold speculations and simple remedies for immense
ills was past, and was desirous of addressing the world with his
mature and selective mind. In spite of that *Queen Mab* took its
way, and if any poem of such length and argument was in the
pocket of the artisan during the early years of Queen Victoria, it
was this.

The meteorology of fame is complex and delightful; and
Shelley was a poet as well as a king of thought. To those who are
acquainted with the volumes of verse, many of them forgotten
now and reduced in number to very few examples, which saw the
light between 1820 and 1840, the influence of his lyrical and
figurative masterpieces on the aspirations of new writers is an
obvious theme. In *Pauline* Robert Browning spoke for a number
of young contemporaries of whose existence he knew nothing.
People with whom Shelley's real or presumed views on the
supreme being and on marriage had no chance could yet find his
poetic nature and voice irresistible; in that respect they had at

their head no less a man, no less conservative a judge of human affairs, than Wordsworth. When Thomas Hood (in 1824 or so) first visited Charles Lamb at his own fireside, he found Wordsworth also sitting there; and many years later what he recollected of the conversation was "a discussion on the value of the promissory notes issued by our younger poets, wherein Wordsworth named Shelley, and Lamb took John Keats for choice".

But, to dwell a moment on the vestiges of Shelley's first effect on the sensitive small-scale poets in that period, I take up one of their books. It is by a young lady whose Christian piety was exemplary, and the title-page reads, "*Lays of Leisure Hours*: by Maria Jane Jewsbury, author of *Letters to the Young*, etc... 1829." At once it reveals the finer intellectual operation for which Shelley had lived; the opening poem is headed *Invocation to the Spirit of Poesy*, and its final stanza is only to be called Shelleyan:

"Then whilst a pilgrim here, celestial stranger,
And though enshrouded, men with rapture view thee,
Whate'er the clime or heart in which a ranger,
Let thy bright home be as a star unto thee,
That with a tongue of fire, doth heavenwards woo thee.
    Wings hast thou?—fold them not in rest supine;
    And incense?—waste it on no human shrine;
An ever-burning lamp?—oh! be its light divine."

It was in 1829 that *Adonais* was republished at Cambridge through the zeal of some undergraduates who believed that Shelley's day had fully dawned.

Still using Miss Jewsbury's book as a single illustration of the spreading of Shelley's fame, I find there a "Poetical Portrait" which, had it been anonymous, some hopeful student would surely have endeavoured to add to the Shelley canon: its stanzas do not require any explicit allusion to their immortal prototype.

". . . A magic scroll unbound
    Seems this world to me;
Beauty strews the ground,
    Beauty gilds the sea,
And I have caught the light all from thine eyes and thee.

Now, if I view a rose,
    Drooped with dew and light,
'Tis like thee, it grows—
    Vision of delight,
Or why hast thou such charms, or I such powers of sight?

In some fair dell hidden
    By night, and cool, and green;
Where sweet things unbidden
    Scatter song and sheen,
All unto eye and ear, speak of thee my queen. . . ."

A poet who has at all times a few and most devoted admirers
has left us a symphonious declaration of what Shelley meant to
followers like himself. T. L. Beddoes was not bothered by doubts
over Shelley's future. It had arrived. At Oxford in 1822 Beddoes
wrote in a blank leaf of *Prometheus Unbound*:

"Write it in gold—A spirit of the sun,
    An intellect ablaze with heavenly thoughts,
    A soul with all the dews of pathos shining,
    Odorous with love, and sweet to silent woe
    With the dark glories of concentrate song,
    Was sphered in mortal earth. Angelic sounds,
    Alive with panting thoughts, sunned the dim world.
    The bright creations of an human heart
    Wrought magic in the bosoms of mankind.
    A flooding summer burst on poetry;
    Of which the crowning sun, the night of beauty,
    The dancing showers, the birds whose anthems wild
    Note after note unbind the enchanted leaves
    Of breaking buds, eve, and the flow of dawn,
    Were centred and condensed in his one name
    As in a providence—and that was SHELLEY."

Historians of the progress of poetry may come at their conclusions by various avenues, and in such instances as Keats and Shelley the thorough exploration of each of these amounts to years of diligence and rows of notebooks. These poets came and in a short time composed their rich collections of poems of all descriptions when the anthologists were multiplying in the land. To make registers of Keats and Shelley in early anthologies—if the range was terminated only with Palgrave and Allingham—would be far beyond the present book and its design. Yet for the least sketch of Shelley's fame one or two typical publications from his age may be within our limits. S. C. Hall's *Book of Gems* (1838), that splendidly arrayed anthology, included the following pieces by Shelley,—*Venice* (from the *Euganean Hills*). *The Cloud, An Exhortation, Mutability, To Night* and *To a Sky-lark*—as well as a page of biography and criticism mainly by Leigh Hunt. The illustration, an appropriate selection, was from a picture of Venice by Bonington. Here perhaps Shelley is seen as he was reaching the wealthier kinds of readers; but in Chambers' *Cyclopædia of English Literature* (1844) he is displayed so that nobody need be without some "piece of him" even if the editors regard his work as precluded from popularity by abstract remoteness and want of simple unity in his designs. "He had, however, many great and shining qualities. . . ." The Chambers selection comprised excerpts from *The Revolt of Islam, The Cenci, Prometheus Unbound, Queen Mab, Alastor, The Sensitive Plant*, with *The Cloud, To a Sky-lark, Stanzas Written in Dejection, Lines to an Indian Air*, and *Music, when soft voices die*. An important choice, for the work was widely circulated.

By 1843 one to whom Shelley's fame was the highest of all considerations had done most of her work in furtherance of it. Mary Shelley undergoes all the mutations of our approval and our antipathy, but will never be deprived of her pre-eminence among the many who have extended our knowledge of what Shelley wrote and what Shelley was. It may be agreed that, brilliant and eloquent as her other works usually were, she never exhibited higher powers of understanding, ordered thought or gracious expression than in the short studies of Shelley which she devised to circumvent the family ban on her bringing out a biography of the poet. Mary was not slow in beginning her great and vital task. Within two years of Shelley's death she published the *Posthumous Poems* with a prefatory memoir, dated 1st June, 1824; and she announced her intention of issuing a companion volume containing the prose remains. Frustrated by the obstinacy of Sir Timothy Shelley, she had to wait until 1839 and 1840 before she could send forth her memorable edition of Shelley's works. In contemplating what she thus achieved for the fame of Shelley, we remember that her publisher Edward Moxon, "a bookseller among poets and a poet among booksellers", had a hand in the achievement. Either she or he had an especially happy thought when it appeared that Shelley's *Minor Poems* would form an excellent pocket volume by themselves.

Between 1824 and 1839 it was principally the opportunity of anthologists to advance Shelley's fame; not many could possess copies of his own editions or of the few things like the Cambridge *Adonais* and the *Masque of Anarchy* published by Leigh Hunt (as he had long before promised the author) in 1832. But the demand for Shelley, the man with the vision, was such as to occasion several ways of getting at his works. The Galignani volume of 1829 in which Coleridge, Keats and Shelley were published together was officially limited to sale on the continent, but copies would hardly fail to come to England. In London the pirates at least supplied the poorer reader, if he wanted Shelley. What came of Benbow's edition (1826) I do not know; John Ascham's (1834) probably got much further; and, as I write, I have by me a copy of the edition in miniature by Charles Daly (1837). It must have been a cheap little book, and the paragraph in the preface defending the inclusion of *Queen Mab* probably tells us what it was that made the non-ruling class call for such editions of Shelley as these. Meanwhile another little book called *The Beauties of Shelley* had passed through three or more editions.

After 1839, however unluckily the question of a biography of Shelley fared, the principal writings of Shelley were before the world, and his name acquired a glory which some incorruptible dissentients have explained as being only luminous paint tastefully and slily applied there by Mary Shelley and her daughter-in-law. These few observations on the growth of Shelley's fame as it recorded itself in the catalogue of books need not be extended much more. The era of modern editing set in, and Shelley was speedily honoured by a series of assiduous scholars among whom W. M. Rossetti was ahead in 1870 with a revised text of the Poems and "the first methodical narrative of the entire life of the poet". Popular issues of Shelley's verse and prose came forth in abundance, and the last date that I shall now give as far as publications are concerned is 1872. In that year *The Poems of Percy Bysshe Shelley* became Vol. 1207 of the Tauchnitz series of British Authors, under the editorship of Mathilde Blind, whose introduction is an act of adoration representative of the feelings of many Shelleyans of that day. The central emotion which they knew, and which will always arise here and there, is suggested by Miss Blind in these words: "If we would in an embodiment of flesh and blood seek for that haunting aspiration which lurks more or less dimly in the minds of all of us; if we would seek for a being in whom the spiritual tendencies completely triumphed over the more material parts of nature; in one word if we would seek the purely human stripped of all its grosser adjuncts and see as in a mirror how little less than angelic it is given to man to be, let us turn with glad eyes and adoring hearts to Percy Bysshe Shelley."

Measure and proof of fame are of other kinds than places in literary selections and new impressions; the bibliographical assessment of Shelley's high repute is incomplete without the notice of translations, of biographies, of critical studies in their diversity. But beyond all this, the fame of Shelley lives in his quality, challenge, and idealism as they inhabit "the general heart of man". People do not always inherit an exact and documentary notion of Shelley, but he has a way of being present to the minds of many who take little heed of printed poetry as the exemplar of the poetic type—a strange man, a wild creature, but in sight of things not for common capabilities, and likely any day to surprise us all with the truth. For Shelley above all, the sense of genius is widespread in relation to what A. N. Whitehead has discerned in him with authority; "a Newton among poets" is bound to have a special name with the scientist who preserves his interest in the possibilities of literature.

I am warned at intervals that Shelley's fame is a waning flame; and sixty years ago when Thomas Hardy was at a bookshop looking for an edition of his honoured poet he was informed (as he mentioned once to me) that Shelley was gradually losing ground, and would presently have none to lose. What brought this talk about I now forget, but I believe it was the enormous prices that had recently been given for first editions of Shelley; at any rate, Hardy's slight reminiscence made him cheerful at one of life's little ironies. Had the bookseller's prediction come true, he would still have maintained that Shelley was death-less and enjoying a sort of anonymous fame in the diffusion of his theory of life and notably of the doctrine of loving-kind-ness.

But still, the cry goes up that Shelley is foundering anew, apparently because he did not perfect his æsthetic equipment; and because a number of us do not like his subjects or his imagery. If the comment is that books and articles upon Shelley have been appearing—in these years so unsuitable for studies, moreover—at an extraordinary rate, so that almost every week produces a new one, it may be countered with the assertion that these are principally by-products, exercises of learning and logic upon accessible materials. Or now and then, to be sure, a new episode is unearthed in what was certainly a biography *bien accidenté*, and the other biographers at once rush to the scene—but what of it?

There is still something to submit as testimony to the survival of Shelley's fame far surpassing the specialist's concerns, and independent of individual objection to a simile or a progressive intellectual theme. One thing is the perpetual recourse of the anthologists to Shelley's book—and it may be allowed that anthologists do not select pieces in which the art of poetry is immature. The other occurs to me as a consequence of my own life-long inability to perceive the decline and impending fall on Shelley's illustrious creation. Many others who have persisted in a similar heresy have been eager to tell me their thoughts on Shelley, either by letter or in conversation. Altogether I am heartened to believe that those who have already arranged a sort of Grammarian's Funeral for Shelley's fame are destined to some such surprise as his merry Cloud springs upon rash judgment in a poem which does not grow tired:

> "I silently laugh at my own cenotaph,—
>   And out of the caverns of rain,
>   Like a child from the womb, like a ghost from the tomb,
>   I arise, and unbuild it again."
>
> EDMUND BLUNDEN.

T H E story of Keats, Shelley and Rome would not be complete without some account of the man of our own time, who, "borne darkly, fearfully afar" over the house where Keats died, gave his life for a Shelleyan ideal of justice and liberty.

Son of an Italian father and an American mother, Lauro de Bosis was born in 1901 and grew to manhood in a home of peace and happiness where the rare spirits of several countries were glad to meet and talk. From both parents he inherited much, notably their love of Shelley of whom Adolfo de Bosis, himself a fine poet, remains the best known Italian translator. That Lauro should be a poet seemed inevitable: that he should be the inheritor of chivalry, courage and unfulfilled renown now seems equally part of the pattern. In spirit and in race he drew upon the best of the Latin heritage and the best of the Anglo-Saxon: Shelley in him met the young men of the Risorgimento. Those in Rome who knew him remember first that he was *semplice e buono*.

His attainments were many. A fine classical scholar, he could talk and write with ease and distinction in French and English: he had grown up in a knowledge of art and literature and he was an athlete and swimmer. With a truly Shelleyan sense of *engagement* went a profound interest in science, in its widest sense, and in the physical universe; his doctor's degree in science at the University of Rome showed something of his pursuit of breadth and balance. It was, nevertheless, for poetry that he knew himself destined.

Among the work achieved in a too short life were several translations from Greek Tragedy including, significantly the *Prometheus Vinctus of Æschylus*, a translation of Sir James Frazer's *Golden Bough* and an anthology of Italian Verse, the latter published posthumously in England, prefaced by a survey of Italian poetry written in scholarly English by the compiler and by a foreword from Dr. G. M. Trevelyan.

Finest of his works was *Icaro*, the lyrical drama, written in

1927, with which he won the Olympic prize at Amsterdam. Its subject was suggested by the poet's mother after reading a sonnet of Philippe Desportes:

> *Il mourut, poursuivant une haute aventure,*
> *Le Ciel, fut son désir, la Mer sa sépulture.*
> *Est-il plus beau dessin, ou plus riche tombeau ?*

The theme of *Icaro*, Man enchained seeking liberty through science, is worked out allegorically in the story of Dædalus the inventor who seeks freedom in flight from the thraldom of his master the tyrant Minos. This is Shelleyan enough, and the consequent loss of Icarus, representing all that the inventor held most dear, brings science and actuality into the relationship in which even before the "atomic age" the Italian poet saw them. Above all the scientist is a forerunner. It is Dædalus who invents and whom the tyrant withholds from flying: it is the next generation which inherits, and the next generation which suffers. Beyond and above the tragedy rises the unconquerable Spirit of Man.

Mr. Blunden's interesting correlation of Shelley with the world of modern thought becomes, perhaps, even more interesting when related to the young Italian poet and scientist who was his heir. Shelley himself had referred to writers, which would for him include scientists, as "companions and forerunners" and added

> "The cloud of mind is discharging its collected lightning and the equilibrium between institutions and opinions is now restoring, or is about to be restored."

This idea of "science advancing over a wide front" (found also, as we have seen, in Keats) is strongly suggested in the passage in *Icaro* wherein Dædalus the Scientist gives his profession of faith:

> "*Tiranni e libertà passano entrambi;*
> *crollano i regni e crollano gli dei.*
> *Solo il pensiero vigilante avanza*
> *e inalza un tempio, la Scienza, a fronte*
> *di cui l'Impero de la terra è nulla.*"

[Tyrants are passing, liberties are numbered,
Falling are the kingdoms, fallen are the gods;
Science alone is waking, Mind is marching—
Temples are towering where the Earth bows low!]

In *Icaro*, which leaps into movement from its first line, the poet sang, as Romain Rolland has remarked, *"le progrès, l'élan vital, dans sa forme individuelle et héroique"*. Interwoven with the theme is a strange and Shelleyan strand of personal prophecy and we see poetry within the poet, getting ever closer to action:

> . . . *Ma il mio sogno—nel centro de la mischia*
> *trarre lo voglio, e sia reale e armato!*
> . . . *e quel che oggi è sogno*
> *per virtù del poeta si fa viva*
> *forza operante, una terrena cosa.*

[But, for my dream, it shall be real and arméd,
Striding about the centre of the fray. . . .
And to-day's dreaming quickens in the poet,—
A life, a driving force, a Power of Earth.]

To Lauro de Bosis, as to many spirited young men, the early days of Fascism seemed to be instinct with progress and *élan vital*. But he was not long deceived. Where so many politicians and shrewd business men were busily discovering enlightenment the poet's vision discovered the darkness beyond. Until 1926 he had never taken an active part in politics. Then, suddenly, he was aware of the process of enslavement. It was no time to dream: the dream must become a "driving force". The darkness was spreading from the minds of the Italian people. He saw that tyranny gathers weight as it goes, and starts from men's refusal in its early stages, to take it seriously. Founding with a few trusted friends an organization known as the *Alleanza Nazionale* he circulated pamphlets wherein his countrymen were urged to look beyond present illusions of Fascism to its fatal consequences, and its inevitable fall.

Political adventure led to exile, but the poet continued his activities abroad, working at one time as a porter in a Paris hotel. Then came news of the arrest, torture and imprisonment of two of his comrades in Rome. At once the dream was armed. He wrote and had printed 400,000 pamphlets addressed to the King and the people of Italy. Then, borrowing money from a friend, he bought an aeroplane, his *Pégase*,[1] and with five hours' experience of solo flying took off from Marseilles for Rome.

On the eve of his flight Lauro de Bosis wrote in French the extraordinary document which was to be his testament to the world and which on his way to the airfield he posted to a journalist friend asking that it be published in the event of his failure to return. It was entitled *L'Histoire de ma Mort*. In it he utters not merely a conviction which has been justified by history but a warning, pointed by example and by sacrifice, of what might yet be born in other lands than Italy and with other names than Fascism.

"I am convinced that Fascism will not fall unless there are a score of young men who will sacrifice their lives to cleanse the minds of the Italians. In the days of the Risorgimento there were thousands of young men ready to give their lives but now there are very few. Why? It is not that their courage or their faith is less than that of their fathers: it is that nobody takes Fascism seriously. All of them, from their leaders downward, foresee its early end and to them it seems out of all proportion to give their lives to put an end to what will fall by itself.

"That is wrong. We must die. I hope that after me many others will follow and that they will succeed in shaking public opinion."

He ends thus:

"If my friend Balbo has done his duty there will be those who are awaiting me. So much the better. I shall be worth more dead than alive."

[1] "*Pégase—c'est le nom de nom de mon avion—a la croupe rousse et les ailes blanches; bien qu'il soit fort comme quatre-vingts chevaux il est svelte comme une hirondelle. Il s'enivre d'essence et bondit dans les cieux comme son frère de jadis, mais, s'il le veut, dans la nuit, il sait glisser dans l'air comme un fantôme.*"

At eight o'clock in the evening of 3rd October, 1931, out of a clear autumn sky, appeared the aeroplane, flying low over the city, circling the de Bosis house as if in salutation, passing over the Piazza di Spagna and after seeming, we are told, "to mount the steps of the Scalinata" turning across the Pincio Gardens and the Villa Borghese. For half an hour the mad flight continued while upon the streets and the gardens, the cafés and the squares there fell from the sky a message of liberty to a people enchained. Then the pilot turned west across the Tyrrhenian Sea and it was not long before the pursuing planes appeared. Over his *Pégase*, as over the *Don Juan* of Shelley, there falls, thereafter, a haze which will never lift.

NEVILLE ROGERS.

THE DEATH MASK OF JOHN KEATS

IN 1948 a lively interest in the Keats world was aroused by the discovery of this cast of the death mask; although why it should have been regarded as a discovery is in itself a minor mystery. The cast, advertised for many years in the trade catalogue of a London firm at trifling cost, appears to have entirely escaped the attention of Keats scholars. When it was brought to my notice I could recall only one possible example which appeared in the Browning Sale Catalogue, 1913, as item 1394 "a plaster Death Mask of Keats". I have, however, since come to the conclusion, from a description of it by Browning in a letter to the Storeys (see *Browning to his American Friends,* edited by Gertrude Reese Hudson, Bowes & Bowes, p. 6) as "my cast from the face of Keats, such a beautiful and characteristic thing" that this was the life mask so often misdescribed. I know now of two other death mask casts (apart from replicas of that given here) one of which, owned by Mr Vivian Meynell, is on loan to the National Portrait Gallery.

The matrix of the mask, taken, perhaps by the Roman mask-maker, Gherardi, the day after Keats died, passed into the hands of his publisher, John Taylor, and at his death was, in 1865 bought by Lord Houghton. We do not know where it is now. No comparison of cast with its matrix being, therefore, possible, a remote doubt as to authenticity must be acknowledged; though apart from the strong resemblance to the life mask, the likeness of later portraits of Keats is marked and further evidence is given by measurements taken with the craniometer of both masks by Professor F. Wood Jones, F.R.S., of the Royal College of Surgeons who, together with Mr. T. B. Layton, D.S.O., M.S., of Guys, has examined the cast. Both gentlemen are of the opinion that "there is nothing incompatible with both masks being of the same man, living or dead".

In comparing the masks readers will notice that, although the face of the dead Keats is emaciated, marked with suffering, the strong mobile mouth has the same slight upward slant, the same hint of humour.

DOROTHY HEWLETT.

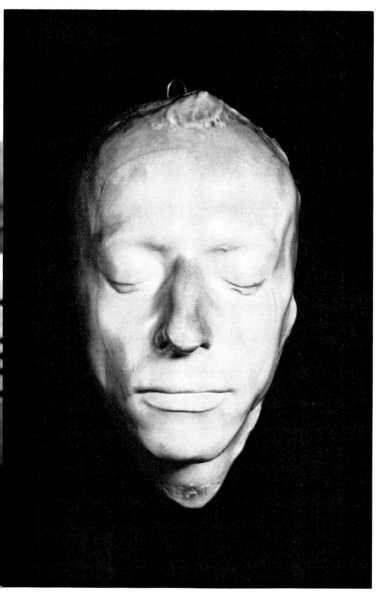

DEATH MASK OF KEATS
(by permission of the owner, copyright not to be reproduced)

THE PIAZZA DI SPAGNA, ROME
from an old print.

THE MEMORIAL

1 9 0 3 — 4 0

FO R initiating the idea of a permanent memorial to Keats and Shelley in Rome[1] first honours must go to America.

During the nineteenth century, despite the fame of the two poets, both the Protestant Cemetery and the Piazza di Spagna suffered their vicissitudes. Attempts made by the Roman municipality to move the remains of Keats and Shelley had frequently to be combated by the British Embassy, and on one occasion were defeated only by the personal intervention of Queen Victoria; there were attempts, also, to drive a wholly unnecessary street through that part of the cemetery which lies between Keats' and Shelléy's graves. About the turn of the century, shortly after the distinguished tenancy of Dr. Axel Munthe of which an account is given in *The Story of San Michele*, the house in the Piazza di Spagna became neglected and was in danger of being absorbed into a big hotel. Municipal vandalism even threatened the removal of the Bernini fountain.

In 1903 eight American writers resident in Rome met to discuss a project for purchasing by popular subscription the house where Keats died, and for installing therein a permanent memorial to Keats and Shelley; this memorial was to consist of a library of their works in various editions, manuscripts and other relics; the trustees at the same time were to have perpetual guardianship over the graves of the two poets and of their friends Severn and Trelawny.

By great good fortune this American enterprise coincided with the presence in Rome as Chargé d'Affaires of the late Lord Rennell of Rodd (then Sir Rennell Rodd). Than this great diplomat and distinguished scholar no more enthusiastic supporter could have been found. Invited to preside over the project he lent his full

---

[1] Keats has his Memorial in England, where his Hampstead home, preserved from destruction in 1920 by local and national endeavour, now reposes with its treasures in the safe care of the Hampstead Corporation. Its preservation owed much to American generosity and to the work of Miss Amy Lowell and her Boston Committee.

weight in the difficult negotiations and by 1906 an option had been secured on the property. King Edward VII and President Theodore Roosevelt signified their sympathy and by private endeavour funds were raised on both sides of the Atlantic.

Three committees were instituted; an Executive Committee in Rome under the ex-officio Chairmanship of the British Ambassador, and Committees in England and America presided over, originally, by Sir Sidney Colvin and Edmund Clarence Stedman respectively. The lists of names in these original committees make imposing reading, and some of those who then worked so hard are no less enthusiastic supporters to-day.

In 1909 the Memorial was opened in the presence of the King of Italy, of the British Ambassador, and of a gathering of British, American and Italian writers. Relics, pictures and manuscripts were generously contributed by the Shelley and Leigh Hunt families, by the Marquess of Crewe (son of Lord Houghton, pioneer among Keats scholars) and by Harry Buxton Forman.

For years the Memorial flourished. Periodical *Keats-Shelley Bulletins*, based on unpublished material in its library, were a valuable contribution to scholarship. That library, meanwhile, grew to contain over 10,000 volumes and soon afforded facilities for the study of Keats and Shelley, as well as of their contemporaries in Italy, Leigh Hunt and Byron, unrivalled anywhere saving perhaps the British Museum. Fulfilled were the hopes of the first Rome Chairman:

> "And therefore men from either side the sea
> Who speak the same great language, joining hands,
> Designed the poet's house of death to be
> A pilgrim shrine for poets of their lands."

For thirty years in a city richer in memorials than any other in the world not only poets but visitors of all kinds, from Britain, from America, and from other countries as well, felt the significance of a memorial worthy of those who speak the tongue of Keats and Shelley. Later events were to increase that significance.

1940–44

The compensating good fortune which blessed both Keats and Shelley with loyal friends while they lived has hitherto continued its blessing since their deaths. Seven years before the shadows fell between England and Italy their Rome Memorial had secured as its Curator Signora Signorelli Cacciatore, a lady whose scholarship is equalled by her courage and resource and who has, moreover, the gift of winning friends both for herself and for the poets she untiringly serves.

When, in 1940, the Italian people were dragged to war the Committee in England were cut off from all direct contact with Rome, and, inevitably, the English members of the Executive Committee in Rome were obliged to leave. For over a year while the United States remained at peace, American Committee-members continued their efforts. Chief of these, in Rome, was the Honorary Secretary Mr. Hale Benton. Foreseeing that with the extension of hostilities he too would sooner or later be obliged to leave Mr. Benton enlisted other "neutral" help, and Dr. Erik Sjöqvist, Director of the Swedish Institute in Rome, undertook the office of Honorary Treasurer.

In the next few years Dr. Sjoqvist proved a pillar of strength. The problems were both political and financial. A wealth of caution and diplomacy was needed to maintain Keats' House as a neutrally-protected concern and to avert Fascist or Nazi intrusion. The circumstances of the war had reduced incoming funds till they were almost negligible. Everything depended on careful husbandry of existing capital. Confident always that liberation must eventually come Curator and Treasurer worked together to eke out that capital till the day when the Allies should reach Rome. It was little enough, and an eighteenth century building needs constant repair. Then on 10th September, 1943, after the Badoglio armistice, the Piazza di Spagna came for several hours under German shell-fire. Neighbouring houses were badly hit, no glass was left in the windows of No. 26 and its roof was badly damaged. Hardly had the repairs been effected when another disaster threatened: partisans attacked and fired an adjacent Fascist headquarters. For some hours, till the fire could be controlled, it seemed that Keats' House was doomed.

E*   67

All this while the chief treasures of the house lay far from Rome. They had gone to what then appeared as safe a place as any in Italy—the Abbey of Monte Cassino. Here again fate and loyal friends intervened for the poets. When the tide of war rolled north of Naples the monks were ordered to evacuate. Many of the Abbey's own treasures fell into the predatory clutches of the Herman Goering division. Nevertheless the two small boxes from the Piazza di Spagna, guarded as jealously by the monks as anything of their own, remained concealed in the cell of the archivist. Later this brave man, Don Mauro Inguanez, had them conveyed back to Rome disguised as his personal baggage. In a German lorry and with an armed guard provided by the looters themselves they duly reached the Piazza di Spagna.

What of the graves in the Protestant Cemetery? Close to the Porta San Paolo lies the Ostia Station, a regular target, during the German occupation of Rome, both for British and for American aircraft. Bombs rained around the cemetery. Several tombs were smashed and a number of pines and cypresses thrown down. But, saving one bomb which damaged the wall between the Pyramid and Keats' grave, nothing came near the resting-place of the poets or their friends, or of William Shelley, and no damage was done to the essential beauty of the plot.

Of the great day when Keats' own language was again heard at his door an account has been given earlier by the first of the Allies to greet the Curator. There follows an account of that day from the Curator herself:

"It was on 4th June 1944 that the Allies entered Rome. All day long there had been a stream of Germans through the City and when at half past nine a voice in the Piazza di Spagna called from the windows that the Allies were coming the people all turned out of their houses.

"Keats' House had long been closed and the door into the Piazza remained fastened even after the tidings from that unknown voice in the dark. It was hours since we had heard a motor-car or a *carrozza* and the cheerful fountain, since the bombing of the conduits, bubbled no more. An unearthly silence reigned under the white round moon. Suddenly came the throb of an engine. A lorry dashed past and a machine-gun began to fire. Amid the crowd a man was seen to fall while others threw themselves hastily to the ground. There was a tinkling of glass and the lorry disappeared. The last German had crossed the Piazza. Everyone had taken cover indoors, two persons excepted. These lay on the ground, one of them dead and one wounded. Next door to Keats' House the dressmaker's window had been smashed into fragments. The square was quiet once more.

"Half an hour later came another cry from a window: the Allied soldiers were in the Via Due Macelli. Already the rumbling of their tanks could be heard.

"There they were at last, marching slowly, in single file, headed by a few tanks. As they enteied the square they split into two columns each following the line of one of the pavements. On went the soldiers like robots; they waved but they did not stop while the people cheering in the moonlight, drowned the noise of their marching. Somebody would flash a torch to look into the face of an Allied soldier: the man would smile but he would not stop. Thus, almost curtly it ·seemed, the first columns went by. After a minute or two others arrived. These were more numerous and made more noise, calling out to each other and turning to joke with the crowd.

"For a quarter of an hour the stream continued like water pouring down a hill. Then an order was given and a halt was made. The Piazza was crowded. Soldiers and civilians jostled together amid a babel of languages. The men begged for water or wine, both the same to them—the fountains were dry and in the houses alone was drink to be had.

"Now they had drunk and lay stretched upon the ground. Within five minutes of the order to halt the Piazza was covered with recumbent figures. There in the moonlight slept the soldiers: on the pavements, in the dried-up fountain, on the Scalinata of Santa Trinità dei Monti, propped against the obelisk; pillowed on a haversack, a kerbstone, a doorstep or a comrade. For one moment it seemed that all these men were dead, victims of a silent battle fought in the Piazza. Civilians would stoop and rouse them and they would reply that they were tired, tired from marching but glad to have reached Rome. Not one of them was aware at the corner of the Scalinata of a little orange-bricked house containing the manuscripts and pictures of one of the greatest poets of their country or knew that that little house had now found security. Still warm with the June sunshine the Piazza had become one huge bed. The civilians who streamed increasingly from their houses could not walk an inch without stepping over the out-stretched bodies, bodies so strangely similar in their khaki uniforms and in the light of the moon that peered from behind the obelisk. Those who had not seen them settling down to rest found themselves shuddering from the nightmare-notion that the Piazza's air had cast a fatal spell over a whole army.

"Then there was life again. A sharp command, and the stream resumed its course. Out of the dry fountain emerged the sleepers, and from the Scalinata's stones awoke men who, a few minutes past, had been fallen statues.

"All night long the soldiers went by. None of them can have seen the house of their poet, indistinguishable from any other in the Piazza since all notices had been taken down in wartime and the marble plaque deliberately neglected; even in daylight the inscription was barely legible which marks the famous place. The night was filled with the sound of tanks and lorries, of armoured cars and of words of command. On 5th June, at six o'clock in the morning, the first Allied visitor knocked at the door of Keats' house. It was Sedgwick the American journalist. He asked, 'Everything all right?' We could tell him that everything was all right.

"The two sealed boxes, which had travelled to the Abbey of Monte Cassino and had returned in one of the Goering Division's lorries, lay wrapped in newspaper under a table. For the first time for years, the windows were open, to let in the dawn of 5th June, 1944. German officers had often asked to enter the house. They were always refused. 'It is closed' the curator would say. 'Strange', they would reply, 'there always seems to be somebody cleaning on the second floor'.

"At dawn on 5th June the Keats-Shelley Memorial emerged from its secret life. Notices drawn up by Allied Headquarters and hung on its outer walls restored an identity to the little eighteenth-century building. That night two armed soldiers went on guard.

"They arrived about eight o'clock when it was getting dark. The Curator asked: 'Have you come for Keats' House?' 'Yes' they replied, speaking together. Then one of them said, 'I am a student. Might I be allowed for one moment to go alone into the room where Keats died?' The student—his name was Leonard Rosenberg—handed his rifle to his companion and with a candle he went up the dark stairway and made his way round the dark rooms once occupied by Keats and Severn. Behind the thick lenses came a gleam in eyes once tired with poring over texts. The Curator asked if the guards had to stay all night in the street or if they would prefer to stand in the doorway.

" 'We take turns,' replied the soldier, Leonard Rosenberg, 'and we will stand in the street. I am proud to be on guard before a poet's house. This is the first time since I went into the Army that I have been ordered to surrender to poetry.' "

VERA SIGNORELLI CACCIATORE

tr. N.R.

1944–46

Within a few weeks of the liberation of Rome the Keats-Shelley Memorial was formally reopened in the presence of the Ambassadors of Great Britain and of the United States of America. Then began an era such as the little house had never known and may never know again.

Before 1939 visitors had reached an annual average of 800; these included tourists as well as the scholars and students who came for research work in the fine library. Now, within one year from its reopening no less than 15,000 visitors appeared, among whom were represented all ranks of British, Dominion and Allied Forces. Many returned again and again, some drawn by the library and the relics, some more simply by a place of peace, which was, in the words then heard so inevitably and so often, "some corner of a foreign field that is for ever England". To those already familiar with the stories of Keats and Shelley the Memorial revealed a new significance; to others it told a story of its own. Thus in war did a home of poetry come to mean more, and to more people, than ever in the old days of peace.

NEVILLE ROGERS.

NOTE ON A DRAWING OF JOHN KEATS

BENJAMIN ROBERT HAYDON (1786–1846) was the English painter who induced his countrymen to buy the Elgin Marbles. His enthusiasm and vitality made a considerable impression on the mind of the young Keats. Well-known in his day as a painter of historical and Scriptural subjects—on canvases, frequently, of vast proportions—he eventually lost popular favour and was driven to suicide. His was a tragedy of misdirected energy. Few reading his *Diary* or his *Autobiography* would fail to agree that his real talent lay less in painting than in literature.

The drawing which faces this page was originally reproduced by permission of the late M. Buxton Forman, former owner of the manuscript of Haydon's *Diary*. Its continued reproduction is kindly permitted by Professor Willard B. Pope, its present owner and Editor. Mr Forman contributed the following note. *Ed.*]

"I dreamt last night of dear Keats. I thought he appeared to me, & said, 'Haydon you promised to make a drawing of my head before I died, & you did not do it. Paint me now.' I awoke, & saw him as distinctly as if it was his spirit. I am convinced such an impression on common minds would have been mistaken for a Ghost. I lay awake for hours dwelling on his remembrance. Dear Keats! I will paint thee—worthily & poetically.

"Ah, Wilson & Lockhart, if Man ever was murdered, it was John Keats—and if ever Men were murderers, ye are they!

"Wilson, when I was in Edingburgh, could not bear his high poetical Genius. His envy, his malice, were apparent. He spoke of him with undisguised malignity."

So wrote Benjamin Robert Haydon in his *Diary* on 14th November, 1831, of Keats and of his reviewers. Directly below the entry he made the rough pen and ink sketch here reproduced. As a portrait of the poet it does not bear comparison with the fine head drawn from life some fifteen years before, but I think it must be allowed that it gives to the poet the same eager expression that characterizes his earlier sketch which is now in the National Portrait Gallery.

M. BUXTON FORMAN.

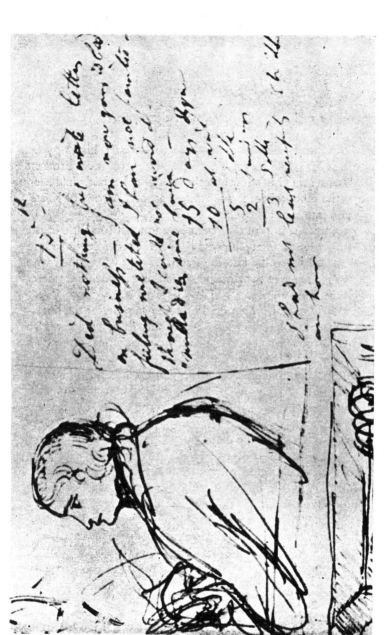

SKETCH OF KEATS BY BENJAMIN ROBERT HAYDON

(by special permission of Prof. Willard B. Pope: copyright: not to be reproduced).

POSTSCRIPT

"IT might make one in love with death, to think that one should be buried in so sweet a place."

So wrote Shelley in the preface to *Adonais*, his elegy on the death of his friend Keats. To this "sweet place" were brought Shelley's own ashes but a few months later after his body had been burnt on the sands where it was washed ashore. A copy of Keats' poems was found in his pocket.

So it comes that two of the youngest and most romantic of the great brotherhood of British poets lie together on foreign soil, in Rome, where lie also the bodies of some of our young men who fell lately in defence of the British way of life, of which our poetry is one of the chief glories.

To the Keats-Shelley Memorial building came, after the liberation of Rome, some 15,000 young men of the Allied armies, drawn by the magic of the two poets and by the peace of the house which commemorates their names.

Both Keats and Shelley were under thirty when they met their death, the former after much suffering from consumption, the latter drowned while sailing his boat on a stormy day. Keats was a man of the people, to whom was granted the vision and music of the great poets. Though he died young, his best work is mature, ripened and shadowed perhaps by the fore-knowledge of early death. Shelley came of an old and famous family, and went to Eton and Oxford. But he never lost the common touch or understanding of the people. He is pre-eminently the poet of brilliant headstrong youth—generous, tempestuous, rash, unwise. Unlike Keats he had yet to mature as a poet. His finest verse was still locked in his gallant heart and vivid imagination, and was lost to the world when that fierce squall upset his boat off the Italian coast.

The existence of the Rome memorial to these poets is threatened by the circumstances of the late war, which swallowed up all available funds. With this book appears an appeal to secure its future. It will be an ill day for our people and the world if such an appeal fails to arouse a fitting response since, as another of our poets who also died too early has written:

"If ever there arise a nation whose people have forgotten poetry or whose poets have forgotten the people . . . they will be a dark patch upon the world."

We are not that yet, thank God, indeed my own view is that the British spirit is still a shining beam in what appears for the moment as a rather gloomy world. And a sense for poetry, often unconscious, is the essence of that spirit.

WAVELL,
F.M.

THE KEATS-SHELLEY MEMORIAL ASSOCIATION

Patron:

HER MAJESTY QUEEN ELIZABETH THE QUEEN MOTHER

President:

EDMUND BLUNDEN

Chairman:

THE RT. HON. THE LORD ABINGER

Hon. Secretary:

NORMAN KILGOUR, Longfield Cottage, Longfield Drive, London, S.W.14

Hon. Treasurer:

THE MANAGER, Barclays Bank (West End Foreign Branch), 1 Pall Mall East, London, S.W.1.

Hon. Editor of the Bulletin

MISS DOROTHY HEWLETT, Longfield Cottage, Longfield Drive, London, S.W.14.

FRIENDS OF THE KEATS-SHELLEY MEMORIAL

In 1950 a body entitled "The Friends of the Keats-Shelley Memorial" was established in order to help to raise funds for a Memorial in Westminster Abbey, for the care of the graves of the poets in the Protestant Cemetery at Rome, and to set up a special endowment for the maintenance of Keats House in Rome.

Two of these objects have already been achieved. We are, still, however, in need of funds for the third object.

"Friends" receive complimentary copies of the Bulletin, Annual Reports and occasional invitations to lectures. The Bulletin, edited by Miss Dorothy Hewlett, the author, makes a special appeal to scholars and has a world-wide circulation. Extra copies and back numbers may be obtained at reduced rates.

The minimum subscription is one guinea per annum, and donors of £100 or over are elected "Honorary Life Members". All enquiries and applications for enrolment as a "Friend" should be addressed to the Hon. Secretary.

KEATS SHELLEY and ROME has been written and compiled for the Keats-Shelley Memorial Association, to which all royalties will be devoted.

ETTORE CUOMO
VIA AURELIA 770   6230452
00165 ROME - ITALY